I'm an 8-Hole

For Enneagram Eights
and Those Who Put
Up With Them

C. V. Meo

©Copyright 2022 by C.V. Meo.

All rights reserved.

No part of this publication may be reproduced, distributed, or transmitted in any form or by any means, including photocopying, recording, or other electronic or mechanical methods, without the prior written permission of the publisher, except in the case of brief quotations embodied in critical reviews and certain other noncommercial uses permitted by copyright law.

All Scripture quotations, unless otherwise indicated, are taken from The Holy Bible, NEW INTERNATIONAL VERSION®, NIV® Copyright© 1973, 1978, 1984, 2011 by Biblica, Inc.™ All rights reserved worldwide.

While any stories in this book are true, some names and identifying information may have been changed or combined to protect the privacy of individuals.

Please note the information contained within this document is for educational and entertainment purposes only. All effort has been executed to present accurate, up-to-date, reliable, and complete information. No warranties of any kind are declared of implied. Readers acknowledge that the author is not engaging in the rendering of legal, financial, medical, or professional advice. Please consult a licensed professional before implementing any of the strategies in this book.

Cover Design and Artwork by Kale Daniels.

ISBN 9798849190495 (print)

Printed in the United States of America.

Library of Congress Cataloging-in-Publication Data
Names: Meo, C.V., 1995- author.
Title: I'm an 8-hole: for enneagram eights and those who put up with them / C.V. Meo
Library of Congress Control Number: 2022916435

I like a man who grins when he fights.
Winston Churchill

CONTENTS

Introduction *1*
Chapter 1 - The B8sics **10**
The Enneagram Eight 11
Core Motivators 17
Core Fears 23
Core Desires 27
Core Weaknesses 30
Chapter 2 - Vari8tions **35**
Wings 36
Subtypes 40
Female Eights 48
Chapter 3 - The Origin Story **51**
The Eight Childhood 52
The Switch 55
Innocence and Nurture 60
Triangulating Our Childhood 67
Denying Our Tears 70
Chapter 4 - Let Me Hear Your Body Talk **75**
The Anger That Protects 76
Your Body Keeps Score 80
Intensity in Everything 84
Befriend Your Body to Befriend Your Heart 88
Chapter 5 - Faith and Eight **92**
Jesus' "Eight" Moment 94
Swords and Revenge 97
Unrighteous Anger 102
The Ultimate Betrayal 104
Be the Last 107

Chapter 6 - How To Not Be a Dick to the Other Eight Numbers **111**
Ones 113
Twos 117
Threes 120
Fours 122
Fives 124
Sixes 127
Sevens 130
Eights 132
Nines 134
Chapter 7 - I Married an Eight **139**
Imprinting 140
Rejecting Rejection 144
Honesty Not Cruelty 146
Conflict With an Eight 147
Eight Tips for Marriage With an Eight 152
Eight Tips for an Eight Who's Married 159
Chapter 8 - The Path Forward **169**
Stress and Security 170
How to Discover Your Triangles 174
How to Be Vulnerable 178
How to Handle Betrayal 189
How to Befriend Your Inner Child 194
Appendix A - Questions for Eights *203*
Appendix B - I Was Raised by an Eight *207*
Appendix C - 88 Imperatives for Eights *213*
Appendix D - Music, Movies, & Famous Eights. *217*
Acknowledgements *225*
References *227*

INTRODUCTION

WELCOME TO THE ENNEAGRAM AND THE EIGHT

The Enneagram can be confusing.

What even is the Enneagram? Is it like Astrology? Is it like the Myers-Briggs test? Is it like one of those Buzzfeed quizzes where they tell you what magical house from Harry Potter you would be placed in?

The answer to those questions is... Yes? No? Maybe? Sometimes?

The Enneagram, put most simply, is an abbreviated way to categorize the different motivational patterns of humanity. In short, there are 9 ways, titled under the numbers 1-9, in which humans are motivated to interact with the world around them. Under each number lies humanities' basic fears, desires, weaknesses, motivations, and longings.

The Enneagram can be backed by psychology. It can be supplemented by sociology. Hell, it can even be supported by religion.

I've found that the Enneagram is more helpful than all of the other personality assessments. This is because the Enneagram focuses on WHY you do what you do, not just on your behaviors. This is so much more helpful than just telling you some basic qualities, communication styles, or activities you might like. It helps you discover how you've come to view and interact with the world in the ways that you do.

Plus, the Enneagram breaks down the 9 numbers into subtypes and wings. With those variations, it is possible to type someone 54 (54!) different ways. Because of this, I have found that the Enneagram can be much more individualized to the wide variety of human experiences.

To further understand the Enneagram, I find it is best to use stories–and this book will have lots of them!

So, I would like to begin with a story about an Ivory Tower.

Once upon a time, in a faraway land, there was an ivory tower.

This tower was beautiful, majestic, and a symbol of hope for the world. Around this tower, humanity formed civilization, community, and customs. And, as with any large group of people, this society naturally fell into certain roles, positions, and factions.

There were nine groups of people that made up this society:

The Threes built the tower. They designed, orchestrated, and architected the tower.

The Twos supported the building of the tower, the functions in the tower, and the other responsibilities of the tower. They often served as servants of the day-to-day and essential activities of the tower.

The Ones sought to live out the tower and its values. They were the ones who lived in a way that honored the tower and encouraged others to do the same.

The Fours beautified the tower. They added art, creativity, and beauty to the tower.

The Phobic Sixes were the most faithful subjects to the tower. Many would call them the best citizens the tower ever had.

The Sevens served as court jesters, party hosts, and facilitators of all events that took place inside the tower. They brought life, excitement, and lightness to the tower.

The Nines were the mediators of the tower. When there was a dispute or conflict, they brought harmony, peace, and resolution to the tower.

As each looked up at the tower, they had different reactions as to its purpose:

The Ones asked, "What's the point of the tower if we don't live like the tower?"
The Twos asked, "What's the point of the tower if it and its people get neglected?"
The Threes didn't ask a question but told those around them, "I'll tell you the purpose of the tower."
The Fours asked, "What's the point of the tower if it's not a place of beauty and creativity?"
The Phobic Sixes asked, "What's the point of the tower if we don't remain faithful to the tower and its values?"
The Sevens asked, "What's the point of the tower if we don't enjoy it and experience it?"
And finally, the Nines asked, "What's the point of the tower if we can't stay harmonized and unified?"

In all of this, cracks started to emerge in the tower. Although it was once perfect, beautiful, and pure, it started to decay. The civilization around the tower also started to crumble. All the different parts of society noticed this happening and sought to fix it in their own unique ways.

With this gap between what the tower stood for and what the current situation was like, the Eights responded to the shortfalls of the tower. They said that "If there was any corruption in the tower, then the whole thing was full of corruption!"

So, the Eights decided to burn the tower to the ground to end the injustice.

With that plan, the Eights recruited the Counterphobic Sixes to help in rebelling against the tower. These Sixes were the best at going against corruption.

As you can imagine, there were some in the other groups that were sympathetic to this cause. However, many were unsure of how to help or which side to join.

The Ones and the Threes sought to keep building the tower because that's where beauty and life could flourish.

The Fours and the Sevens largely stayed out of the dilemma and continued to focus on their fun, beauty, and experiences.

The Twos, Phobic Sixes, and Nines stayed in their positions hoping that this would all be over soon so that they could get back to everyday life.

As this was unfolding, there stood a few on the outskirts of town near a remote cave. These Fives watched as the battle for the tower wore on. They saw the good in each side, the bad in each side, the potential for justice, and the potential for calamity. They watched with great intention. However, they decided that there was nothing they could do to help the tower. Feeling dejected, they slowly retreated back into their cave and dreamed of a world where maybe we wouldn't need a tower at all.

Ages after this battle took place, a famous poet, Enneas, wrote about the tower:

"Ones embody the tower
Twos support the tower
Threes build the tower
Fours beautify the tower
Fives watch the tower
Phobic Sixes are loyal to the tower
Counterphobic Sixes rebel against the tower
Sevens enliven the tower
Eights reject the tower
Nines bring peace to the tower"

This is the story of the Ivory Tower.

If you want to learn more about all that the Enneagram is: the wings, the triads, the subtypes, the stress and security numbers, you can check my references section for resource recommendations. Nonetheless, this is a book only about those fiery Eights.

What is an Eight? What are Eights like? Are all Eights control-freaks? Is my angry boss an Eight? Why do you often have to apologize after telling someone you're an Eight? Why do I hate Eights? Why do people hate me because I'm an Eight?

These are questions I've been asking since finding out about the Enneagram and my identification with the Eight.

I remember my very first experience with the Enneagram like it was yesterday.

I was standing on the upper deck of a ferry traveling from Bainbridge Island back over to Seattle, Washington. I was taking in the sights of the beautiful Puget Sound when I overheard my group of friends talking about these random numbers. I had previously heard about this new personality trend that these white people couldn't shut up about.

Before I get an angry email, chill out white people. I'm white too.

Well, somewhat. I'm actually Sicilian. If you didn't know, Sicilians weren't always considered white in this country, so most of my family history identifies with not being white. But, all of that talk about whiteness is for another book. You can go read about it yourself–like in David Roediger's *Working Toward Whiteness*.

Back to the story…

So, I did what any Eight would do, and loudly proclaimed to my friends that the Enneagram was a "heaping pile of shit." How could a number accurately describe a complex individual with a unique story? It seemed like some horoscopic nonsense.

This led to an uproar around me, with each person trying to validate their foolish attempt to box people in. However, one of my trusted friends, we'll call him "Five", pulled me aside and showed me some of the merits of this typing system. Seeing the usefulness of this system, I then did the next thing an Eight would do.

I asked them directly, "Okay, so then what number do you all think I am?"

Without skipping a beat, my other friend, we'll call him "Six", chimed in and said "You're the Eight. It's the asshole." With that, I looked "Six" squarely in the eye and said "Well, fuck you too then."

Look, I get it.

You might hate the Enneagram. You don't want people putting you in a numerical box. You're tired of people assuming you're an asshole because of this broad generalization. You're tired of people that think you want to be fought on every single damn thing because a stupid number told them to.

I'm sick of it too. Really fucking sick of it.

People don't get us Eights. And if they do understand bits of the Eight, they often use it as weapons against us.

But, just as "Five" did for me in later explaining to me the beauty, innocence, and courage of the Eight, I hope to do the same for you. We are not just variations of the worst dictators in history like Benito Mussolini and Adolf Hitler (Hitler was probably a One anyway).

I am going to ask you to trust me here. I know trust isn't our strong suit as Eights but damn it, just pretend like you do anyway.

This language of personality might actually be something helpful. It might be something you can find hope and freedom in. It might unlock broken pieces of your life. It may even help you not cuss someone out when they backstab you during a game of *Settlers of Catan*. Just maybe.

However, I would also guess that if you're reading this book, then you've at least experienced some of the helpfulness of the Enneagram. If that's the case, my job is much easier.

Or, you might also be a non-Eight trying to understand your friend, partner, colleague, or enemy who is an Eight. If that's you–welcome. I'm glad you're here–be prepared to throw everything you thought you knew about Eights out the door. A lot of it is probably unhelpful or incomplete. And the stuff that's true, well, it's probably still misguided in how you're perceiving your Eight person.

In this book, you will see me change from referring to Eights as "they" and other times as "we." My intention of this book is to write "for Eights by an Eight in Eight language, with others watching in," which requires me to use different pronouns.

Many Enneagram blogs and books are from others' points of view on the Eight, which generally leads to trash descriptions of Eights. Enough of that.

In this book, I will embody an average, typical Eight in my writing. Due to this, I might be a little more brash, haughty, offensive, antagonistic, and vulgar than I actually am in real life. Healthy and self-aware Eights will look different than this. Sorry not sorry.

Regardless, there will also be a lot of swearing and vulgarity in this book. Lots of it. A fucking shit ton of it.

For those who don't understand the beauty and art form of using a good swear word, you will hate it.

For those who view swearing as an essential tool to get a visceral reaction out of people, you will love it.

There are times that even my own language in this book generates a visceral reaction in me. Deal with it.

I try not to overdo swearing as Eights love intentional swearing but hey, nobody's perfect. I'm sure as hell not claiming to be.

With all that said, let's begin our journey of understanding these beautiful, vengeful, strong, angry, generous, passionate, and big-hearted humans.

CHAPTER ONE

THE B8SICS

Before we can dive into all the specifics of what it means to be an Eight, we should acknowledge that each individual human is just that: an individual human.

Sometimes, the Enneagram can be used by people to avoid treating each other with compassion and humility. People use the Enneagram to excuse their stereotypes and judgments about people.

This is *not* how to use the Enneagram.

The Enneagram should be primarily used to discover yourself. This personality system is a tool used to discover your shadow side and blind spots. It should help you dive underneath your behaviors and find why you do what you do.

Self-discovery and growth are the goal. This can be one of many tools that you use to become a more holistic person.

It can also be used to grow your compassion and empathy for others. The Enneagram should lead you out of judgmental thoughts and into curious thoughts. It should prompt you to explore the motivations behind someone's actions, rather than assuming they're just a terrible person.

This book will be a deep exploration in generalities. There will be moments when this book describes your existence down to the letter. There will be other moments where you do not relate to it at all.

When the descriptions below don't fit you, that's okay. Throw them away. Keep what is helpful, discard what is not.

Again, the Enneagram is just an abbreviated way of talking about complex personality generalities. Just like when we use the single word "depression" to describe a complex human experience, the Enneagram does the same thing with personality characteristics.

For me and many other Eights, the Enneagram has been the one personality test that has resonated with us. Horoscopes seem too random, StrengthsFinder seems too positive, and other personality tests don't quite hit the mark.

But, the Enneagram can expose us. This typing system understands us. This one explains us. For those of you who read this book. I hope it provides language, understanding, and tools for self-discovery. The Enneagram has truly revolutionized how I relate to myself and the world around me.

With that in mind, let's establish a baseline of what the Eight is.

The Enneagram Eight

The Eight is often referred to as "The Challenger."

Others have called Eights "protectors, defenders, and contrarians." Fun names right?

Eights are honest, fun, generous, and effective. They value competence, influence, power, and control.

Eights are the most authentic type of the whole Enneagram—sorry Enneagram Fours, you can be the second most authentic type— what you see is truly what you get with an Eight.

Inner integrity is huge for Eights. They want to be the same on the outside as they are on the inside. Because of this, you will never have to wonder what an Eight is thinking or feeling, they'll just tell you.

Since Eights also value inner integrity in their friends, you will have to be mindful about any hypocrisies or contradictions in your own life. If you don't, the Eight will call them out.

Eights have a "bullshit detector" built into their DNA. This is why Eights are extremely attuned to when they are being manipulated or gaslit. Eights refuse to live in places of deceit or dishonesty.

Beyond this, Eights are the most misunderstood type on the whole Enneagram. One of the biggest misunderstandings is in regard to Eights and leadership.

A common misconception is that Eights HAVE to lead or be in charge. This simply isn't true. The Eight's main concern is that someone competent IS leading. They don't have to lead, but it will stress them out if nobody is leading or if someone is not leading well. As a reaction to this stress, they will take control and leadership.

Respect is especially a huge deal for Eights.

A common refrain from Eights is "You don't have to love me or like me, but you WILL respect me." If they don't respect you or feel you don't respect them, it will be very hard for them to interact with you in any tangible way.

Eights often feel the need to get big and take the most direct route to getting what they need. They are the most intense type on the Enneagram and frequently feel invincible. They don't fear failure unless that failure makes them appear weak.

Since Eights are future oriented, they are big picture people and love to have a grand vision for their world. They are constantly looking ahead to future challenges, obstacles, and goals.

A common thought from an Eight is, "I have to deal with this head on." I can't tell you how much time I have spent thinking about the future realities I will have to confront: future arguments I will get into, future plans I have, and future projects I will start. It's a lot of time. Like, A LOT. Way more time than writing this book.

As for more of the basics, Eights have a fundamental need to "be against." Against you. Against an idea. Against some formidable foe. Against themselves while working out. Against your ridiculous choice of favorite movie or best coffee. Against their friends in an eating contest to see how many chicken wings they can eat. Against literally anything.

You might be wondering, "What is this need to be against? Why do Eights have to be this way?"

Well, let me tell you.

The need to be against is rooted in the Eight's sense of safety. If you take into consideration the "fight, flight, freeze" responses of fear, Eights are "fight" types. So, Eights have learned to find safety when they go up against something or someone. It helps them test the thing to see if it is safe for them to be around, which in turn makes them feel safe.

An image might be helpful here: Imagine an Eight enters into an old, creaky, and rundown house. The first thing they might do is test out the walls and foundation of the house by pushing against them. If the walls stand firm, then the house is safe. If the walls crumble, then they need to get the hell out of there. But, the only way to truly find out if the house is safe is to push against it.

In the same way, Eights push against the walls of life to figure out their levels of safety.

Because of this need to "be against," Eights come across as intimidating to others. However, Eights don't realize they intimidate others. For Eights, why would others be intimidated by them if they are not intimidated by themselves?

In connection with their need to "be against," Eights constantly end up in conflict. For an Eight, conflict helps them feel alive. It fires energy through their bones.

Sometimes, I'll pick a fight just simply because I'm bored.

Before you say anything, no, it's not "toxic" at all. Back the fuck off. Do you want to fight me about it?!

However, one huge misconception is that Eights love all conflict.

Sure, play fights are super fun for Eights. Arguing about why *La La Land* was a terrible movie with a terrible message? Fantastic fun for them. Getting into a shouting match about whether a hotdog is a sandwich or not? Inject that shit into my veins.

But, actual conflict? Not their favorite. They are just the type most willing to engage in conflict. Letting conflict simmer for Eights is much harder for them than addressing it head on.

As a child, Eights learned they needed to get powerful and deny weakness. Because of this, they often feel like they can make their own rules and limitations. Eights view rules as suggestions rather than mandates.

As my high school basketball coach once said, "The player across from you wakes up every morning and puts his pants on the same way you do." For Eights, every rule was created by a human just like them.

Who says that any rules are divine? Who has any right to enforce rules made by others? Why the hell does everyone follow man-made rules blindly?

Eights are truly the most rebellious type on the Enneagram.

Because of this, Eights relate to power very differently than most people.

Eights believe the world is divided into the weak and the strong, with them obviously identifying with the strong. For Eights, "might is right." Their roles as adults generally center around these variables.

When Eights walk into a room, they will immediately size up everyone in the space.

Who's in charge? Who's got the most social capital here? Who's dominating the energy of this space? Who's the host here? Who do I need to be wary of? Who can I truly trust here?

It's almost second nature to Eights to be aware of power dynamics. I guarantee if you ask any Eight to gaze over a room, they can give you their answers to those questions above, even if they're just pulling things out of their ass.

This all relates to Eights being gut (body) types.
In the Enneagram, there's this whole thing called "triads" where each of the nine numbers is grouped in threes. For Eights, they are in the gut triad. I don't have time (nor do I honestly care) to explain the ins and outs of each of the triads. You can check out any of the books in the references section to learn more about the triads. As for Eights, we will talk about our bodies and guts in chapter 4.

Continuing, Eights are known to be heroic-like figures with direct access to their anger. An Eight's anger often arises when they feel something unjust has happened or if they feel out of control. With this anger, Eights will normally express it right away. Their anger fuels their pursuit of justice. They seek to exert their will and power onto others in order to bring about justice.

Speaking of power, Enneagram expert Beatrice Chestnut describes the superpower of the Eight as "superpower." Pretty badass right?

This superpower can often lead to Eights overestimating themselves. Their uber self-confidence can skew their view of reality.

When Eights watch different athletes, celebrities, or successful businesspeople on TV, they will often boast, "I can do that. Easy." Eights genuinely believe that if they set their mind and time to something, they will be able to accomplish it. No matter what it is.

However, this superpower usually came at a cost. Growing up, Eights had to be tougher than they actually were. Their childhood was accelerated. Before they knew it, they were acting and behaving like adults.

For many Eights, there was abuse or neglect in their childhood. Their hard, confident, and strong exterior is rooted in these childhood memories. There's so much more to say on this specific reality, but we'll dive into that childhood shit in chapter 3.

With this wounding from childhood, Eights want to be "the voice for the voiceless." This is rooted in their desire to protect the vulnerable parts of themselves, but can take Eights to great heights in helping the world's powerless.

Finally, Eights are generally "feeling" repressed. In one of the triads of the Enneagram, there are 3 centers of existence with "feeling, doing, and thinking." For Eights, they are "doing" dominant with some access to "thinking". Because of this, it will be important for Eights to get back in touch with their hearts and their feelings. More on that later.

So, there's your snapshot of the Eight. Pretty fucking awesome right?

However, I understand people like seeing more concise and specifically sectioned off descriptions of the type. So, we'll do that here too.

Each Enneagram type has some core motivations, fears, desires, and weaknesses.

As you will see, a lot of these motivators, fears, desires, and weaknesses flow into one another. They are not detached internal realities but rather an interconnected web.

Each of these are essential to be understood before we get into the trenches of what it means to be an Eight.

One last quick note: these generalities are about average Eights. Healthy, self-reflective, mature Eights will look slightly or very different. Insecure Eights will also look different. But, we will talk about that in chapter 8.

With that, let's talk about the core motivations of an Eight.

Core Motivators

Eights might be some of the most motivated people you have ever met.

Between full time jobs, side hustles, and passion projects, Eights are often taking on multiple things at once.

As with all Eights, they are extremely passionate about what they want. Due to this, it is extremely hard to get Eights to do something they don't want to do. It is super helpful for partners and colleagues of Eights to understand this and try to discover some of their core motivations.

In this next section, we will explore three of the main motivators of Eights.

To Prove Their Independence and Strength

Although the Enneagram Four is known as the classic individualist, the Eight is truly the rugged individualist of the Enneagram.

They stand alone. Literally, physically, and emotionally, Eights standalone from others.

Eights desperately want to be independent (to protect themselves) and not be indebted to any person or place. Eights believe that depending on others will lead to harm, so they learn to depend on nobody but themselves and their strength.

Because of this, Eights rebel against societal, familial, and cultural norms. They will defy social conventions and social shaming in order to prove themselves and their strength.

You might hear an Eight remark "I don't give a shit what others think about me, all I care about is what I think about myself." Although this may sound strong, it's really a defense mechanism against the pain that others' opinions might bring.

But don't get it twisted, Eights are still extremely tough. Probably some of the toughest people you will ever meet. Most Eights will deny physical pain even exists in their body at all.
To illustrate this, let me tell you a story about middle-school me.

It was eighth grade, and I was in gym class. As with any suburban, young, boys' gym class, there was a lot of messing around.

One of the class's favorite things to do was give "titty twisters" or "five stars" as hard as you could.

Why was this? I have no fucking clue. But, it is what it is.

Regardless, I learned after the first few weeks that if you reacted strongly to the pain, you would just invite more pain from the group. They loved to pick on those it hurt the most.

I specifically remember one day when a bigger kid came over and decided to pinch and twist me as hard as he could. Instead of shying away or hitting him back, I simply stared him straight in his eyes and yelled at him, "Come on, harder! I don't feel a thing. HARDER!"

Needless to say, the group didn't attempt to hurt me after that.

However, no matter how much an Eight convinces themselves they don't feel pain, they do. Especially emotional pain. This might be the greatest fear of them all: emotional pain and betrayal.

The Eight deals with this in an interesting way: denial.

They deny they were hurt. They deny pain. Deny sadness. Deny. Deny. Deny.

Denial is the Eight's best defense mechanism.

But, we will touch on that emotional pain and need to protect ourselves later.

Eights also want to show their strength and put it on display for all to see. Due to this, Eights often have what I call "memory amplification."

Memory amplification is when Eights are recounting a memory, a past story, or some accomplishment of theirs.

What generally happens is that Eights skew the memory to make them appear bigger, stronger, or more grandiose than they actually are. Eights can confuse objective reality with their own personal amplified sense of what's true. The hard part with this is that Eights do this subconsciously. They truly don't realize they are doing this.

If you've ever been in a close relationship with an Eight, you can usually see this happen in real time.

As Eights continue to recount memories, they might slowly uptick the drama or bigness of the memory each time. Soon, Eights lose track of what the actual memory was and end up believing their amplification IS the truth.

To illustrate this, I will use an example from ~~former~~ current evangelical megachurch pastor, Mark Driscoll.

Driscoll, a prototypical Eight, was addressing a room of fellow pastors about the keys to his success. With this added motivation of the crowd, he amplified his memory of his accomplishments. Without blinking an eye, he claimed that he reads "365 books a year."

Is this true? Hell no. Not that a human might be incapable of that and not that Driscoll doesn't 100% believe it, but it's just an Eight inflating himself without realizing it.

He probably does read A LOT of books. Most Eights are very productive, more than the average person. But, Eights also have memory amplification and will boost their stories to impress others with their strength.

However, be wary of challenging an Eight on their memories. They will not like that. And they definitely won't admit they are wrong.

We'll talk more about the Eights' weaknesses later.

To Dominate Their Environment

In the body triad, Eights are very conscious of their environment's effect on them.

Like Ones and Nines, Eights refuse to be affected by their environment.

For Eights, the truth is what they say it is. They will dictate the reality of the world they live in.

Eights also want to make their mark on the world. If you know an Eight, they may have tons of influence among their peers, workplaces, or families.

Much of this impact comes from the Eight's determination to not be influenced by the world. They must dominate their world in order to protect themselves, which leads to them having large impacts on the world around them.

To illustrate this, Enneagram coach Beth McCord describes Eights as huge snowplows.

In snowstorms and treacherous conditions, Eights are the best people to have around you. They will clear out your street plus all the surrounding streets so that everyone can walk and drive safely. However, if you happen to find yourself accidentally in front of the snowplow while it's going, they will destroy you.

Eights view the world as a battleground where people take advantage of each other. In their life, they don't want to be caught unprepared for the battles at hand. So, they rise to the occasion and dominate the world around them.

However, this domination mentality is not rooted in an actual desire to dominate. This motivation goes much deeper. Eights' motivation to dominate stems from their desire to protect themselves.

We'll dive into this more in the "Core Desires" section as we explore control.

To Resist Weakness

This one is fun.

Eights will often go out of their way to cover their weak spots. Whether it's not admitting they were wrong about an argument, avoiding playing games they're bad at, or just simply denying the smaller sides of themselves. Eights will not admit weakness. We simply can't. There's too much at stake.

Eights automatically become big when faced with challenges. In stressful situations, you might see an Eight appear bigger and stronger than you know them to be. They rise to the occasion, rather than crumbling with the pressure. Their weaknesses shrink when the pressure grows.

For me, resisting weakness comes out in my hatred of losing. I honestly don't care if I win games, but it will be the bane of my existence to lose. I literally will cheat (if I won't get caught) to avoid losing. I cannot handle losing. I would honestly rather tie, and I hate tying.

Because of this need to resist weakness, you will lose any argument you get into with an Eight. Not because you are wrong, but simply because the Eight will not back down until you do. They just can't. Admitting we are wrong is too hard to do. Letting you have the last word or upper hand is too unbearable. This might be where the stubbornness of the Eight comes out most clearly. We will literally not back down from any fight. And once we're in the fight, we will not back out until you do first.

In terms of other's weaknesses, Eights can sense them like a shark smells blood. They might point them out directly. They might mock and scorn them. They might expose you in front of a large group.

Since Eights deny weakness in themselves, they also expect you to deny your own weaknesses. For an Eight, it's get big or get out.

I'm sure all of our partners absolutely love this attribute of ours. We will talk more about Eights and their partners in chapter 7.

One of the other ways Eights resist weakness is through denial of undesired emotions. Eights are chronic anxiety, depression, and emotion dismissers.

It can get bad when Eights deny these emotions. I know many Eights that started having panic attacks in their 20's and 30's even though many around them would have never guessed they struggled with anxiety. This is definitely true of my own story as well.

Regardless of what weaknesses Eights try to deny, they have them. They're there.

Core Fears

Many Eights will tell you they have no fears.

What's crazy about that, is that many of them actually believe it. I know I did. I know many of my Eight friends do.
But, as with all of humanity for all of history, Eights have fears too. No matter how hard they try to deny them, they do.

Each Eight has their own specific fears. Fears rooted in childhood. Fears rooted in trauma. Fears rooted in life experiences. Fears rooted in one of their deficiencies. Fear.

We'll talk about two meta-fears here.

Being Harmed or Betrayed

This fear is hard for most Eights to admit.

There's normally painful stories and memories behind this fear. Eights do have extremely tough skin, unless it revolves around what they perceive as betrayal.

In chapter 3, we dive into the origin story of Eights and explore these hurtful memories. But for now, just know that Eights are terrified of betrayal.

Eights have a "betrayal-lens" with which they view the world. They constantly are looking for signs of betrayal. The slightest offense can feel like absolute betrayal to them if it triggers their story. Betrayal can happen on a daily basis for some Eights.

For others reading this, you might be wondering, "What does betrayal look like for an Eight?"

Sometimes, it looks like judging the Eight before you take the time to know them. Other times, it looks like hurting them in a way that they've been deeply hurt before. In other cases, it looks like when you misunderstand them and assume false motivations about them.

If you've ever extremely hurt an Eight with something you thought was minor, this is probably what happened: you hurt them in the way they were deeply hurt as a child. You hurt them in a way that felt like betrayal.

If an Eight is seriously betrayed, that is often the end of the friendship, relationship, or partnership. Eights are one of the most forgiving types on the Enneagram, but not when it comes to this. It might be the thing they are most scared of in this world: being betrayed by those closest to them.

I'm sure I don't need to flesh out exactly what kinds of behaviors this fear will lead to, but we will explore more actions from this fear later on.

Being Controlled by Others

This is one of those areas where Eights are most misunderstood by those who are familiar with the Enneagram.

The common refrain about Eights is that "Eights want to control you." Although this isn't completely wrong, it misses the "why" of why Eights look controlling.

It is not that Eights want to *control you;* they just don't want to be *controlled by you.*

Obviously, the behaviors of this fear can look the same. But, the origin of Eights controlling bent is super important for understanding an Eight. There is an enormous difference between these two motivations for control.

Eights learned at a young age that the world outside of them was unsafe. Because of this, they learned ways of finding safety that showed up in dominance, aggression, and taking charge.

Eights are afraid that if others control the situation, they will get hurt.

Let me say that again because it's important.

Eights are afraid that if others control the situation, they will get hurt.

Most Eights would love for someone else to lead, but they are scared that they will get hurt if they're not leading. Eights are typically great followers of leaders they trust or of leaders that they know are smarter than them (talking about you, Fives). When an Eight isn't in control of their own life, that is when they can truly be harmed, betrayed, or abandoned.

With this fear, Eights are constantly sizing up people to see if they can trust them. They desperately want to feel safe with others but are terrified of admitting that to anyone. So, they usually resort to other means of testing people instead of facing their fears.

For me, like most Eights, we have fun ways of testing those around us.

One of my favorite ways of testing people involves swearing (as you can imagine).

When I would be in a new place with new friends, I would want to see who's safe and who's not. But, how do you do that? How can you figure that out quickly? You can't run a background check or conduct an interview with every person while you're at a house party. So, how do we figure out who we can trust and who we can't?

It's simple, really.

Within about 5 minutes of engaging in conversation with a new person, I would drop a "fuck" and then watch their reaction. If their eyes went wide and they were caught off guard, that person is unsafe. If the "fuck" didn't faze them, then that person might be safe. The logic here is that if you can't handle my "fuck" then you won't be able to handle the rest of me.

Isn't that ingenious? My friends love bringing me around to parties, especially family dinners.

If you have ever met an Eight, there is a high chance that they have a mouth like a sailor–granted, some Eights might be extremely against swearing. For those of you, I am sorry about the language in this book. However, most of you are foul mouthed.

Swear words just flow right out of Eights. Vulgarity is their passion. All of this obscenity is mostly just a way for Eights to test those around them and "be bad." But, sometimes, it's also just because Eights really don't follow social norms as they refuse to be controlled by the masses.

As we will see later, Eights fear being controlled because they are afraid of being powerless.

Core Desires

Eights have many desires. Sometimes too many.

If you've ever been in a close relationship with an Eight, you might be overwhelmed by their passion and grand desires.

We'll talk later about the many, many, desires Eights have, but we will focus on two of the main ones here.

To Protect Themselves and Others

Often heralded as the champions of justice, Eights' desire to protect others (and themselves) is on display for all to see.

This desire leads to many Eights becoming social justice advocates, non-profit employees, and on the front lines of activism. Eights fight for the underdog.

Eights are also very territorial: territorial about their own space, territorial about those they love, and territorial about those vulnerable near them. If you've ever earned the love and dedication of an Eight, you have probably seen this territorial nature come out when they seek to protect you.

The Eight is the friend you send to fight your bullies.

What many don't realize is that the Eights' great effort to protect those that are vulnerable is actually a projection of their deep desire for someone to protect them and their vulnerable parts. They become the protector they never had. They become the thing their childhood self needed. They attack the bullies that beat them up when they were younger.

At an early age, Eights learned that you need to have persistence, perseverance, strength, will, endurance, and bravado in order to survive this world. With this belief, they look for those who cannot survive this world and become their heroes to rescue them from impending harm.

There's a moment from my time playing competitive basketball that has stuck with me ever since.

When I was 14 years old, I was playing in a tournament for my school. At this point in time, I was a very good basketball player but still growing into my confidence as a person.
In this particular game, there was this one kid on the other team who was an absolute pest. He shit-talked me all game and was constantly up in my face.

Since the trash talking didn't work against me, he ramped up his game to become physical with me. All game long he was pushing me, shoving me, and taking cheap shots whenever the referees weren't looking.

It got so bad that the kid came up from behind me and pretended to swing at the ball and slapped me straight in the face. Luckily, the referees called a foul.

But, I wanted more.

I can remember looking at the referee, with tears welling up in my eyes, and yelled, "DO SOMETHING, EJECT THIS KID." But all the referee did was look back at me, shrug his shoulders, and mouth "what do you want me to do about it?"

At that moment, I knew I was on my own for the rest of the game.

Years later, this memory is still burned into my brain.

As an adult, I realize that this random memory stuck with me because it mirrored my own life's existence. I desperately wanted an adult or someone older than me to protect me from the harms of this world. However, all I got were authority figures who turned away or shrugged their shoulders in helplessness.

Because of this reality, Eights became the very thing their childhood self needed: someone who would protect them from the unsafe and dangerous world that seeks to betray and harm them.

For Eights, it's a dog-eat-dog world out there.

Because of this, Eights have a small inner circle. There are normally only a few people that Eights will share their tender sides with.

If you've made it into the inner circle of an Eight, congrats. Don't fuck it up.

To Control Their Own Destiny

This desire is very interconnected with the first desire.

If Eights can control their own destiny, then they will be able to protect themselves and those they care about. If they cannot, it's chaos.

This desire is why you will usually see Eights in leadership positions. Their tenacity, perseverance, and charisma often lead them into powerful positions.

Eights are worshiped when they make it to positions of power, but can easily become the thorn in the sides of their bosses as they climb the ranks. They can be the hardest working, most efficient, and faithful workers on the team, or they can destroy anyone in their path to the top.

Controlling their own destiny also leads to how Eights deal with conflict.

Eights hate beating around the bush and would rather confront things directly. When Eights confront people, it's often to discover someone's true motives behind what they are doing or saying. They want to find out what is behind people's facades, and they will poke endlessly to figure that out.

Ultimately, both of these desires are rooted in the Eight's fundamental distrust of their environment's safety. For Eights, it's crucial to discover where this distrust came from.

Luckily for you, I have included a whole chapter on this in chapter 3 focusing on the Eight's origin story.

Core Weaknesses

If you've ever read anything about the Eight, you will see this word come up again and again: Vulnerability.

Although that is not the only weakness of the Eight–and mind you, there are many–it will be the first of two we explore here.

Vulnerability

Vulnerability. Not transparency, vulnerability. Eights are great at transparency.

We can share with you the worst thing we've ever done without blinking an eye. We can give you the goriest, nastiest, and most shameful details of our lives like we're telling you what we had for lunch. We can tell you that we once took a shit in a parking lot at midnight with absolutely no shame (this totally didn't happen on October 3rd, 2021, in Seattle, Washington). We actually enjoy the look of horror on your face as we share the shadier sides of our lives.

But, that's just transparency. People actually will mistake the Eight's transparency for vulnerability. We can tell you things that have already happened. Things we've already processed. Things we've already worked through. Things we don't view as that meaningful or shameful anymore.

However, we struggle deeply with vulnerability. Although vulnerability is a buzz word for Millennials and Gen Zers, most don't actually understand what it is.

Vulnerability is *experiencing the current possibility of being harmed emotionally or physically.*

Vulnerability happens in the present. Vulnerability is feeling shame, fear, helplessness, or any other undesired feeling in front of others. Transparency is sharing what has already been worked through, vulnerability is sharing what has not.

This is what terrifies us. Eights are terrified of being vulnerable. Eights are horrified at sharing current information or stories that someone could use to hurt them. They feel the same way about showing emotions that others could use against them.

When faced with sadness or other undesired emotions, Eights typically will tell themselves "I don't have time to feel this way. I have things I need to get done right now. I will feel this later." The problem is, they hardly ever get around to feeling because they find more things that need to get done.

Eights actually hate their softer feelings. This is why they will demean and mock those who are more sensitive. It is really a judgment against their own softer side projected onto others. A judgment that's rooted in their childhood.

Eights are constantly mindful of avoiding situations where they are weak or powerless. This is why they come across as strong and aggressive.

It's like an animal backed into a corner and realizing the only way to escape this helpless feeling is to fight back. They are truly scared of letting their inner child come out because they are scared you will hurt the fragile child.

A helpful image for understanding this about the Eight is an image of a wounded boxer in a fight. If a boxer realizes they got one side of their ribs broken, they will protect that side as they continue the fight. They will punch back and hope to hurt you bad enough in order to protect their wounded side. Their defense of their broken side comes out as attacks to immobilize you.

In the same way, the Eight protects their wounded heart in this way. They will attack your weaknesses in order to protect their own.

This is the great fear of the Eight. To be in a state of helplessness and weakness. To be vulnerable.

Beyond vulnerability, there is one other dominant weakness of the Eight.

This weakness is usually described as the Eight's deadly sin.

Lust and Excess

A common saying among Eights sums up this aspect of them nicely: "If anything is worth doing, it's worth overdoing."

Whether it's working out, eating delicious food, starting projects, or seeking out vengeance, Eights frequently overdo just about everything. This overdoing often comes out in the Eight's treatment of their own body, but we'll dive into that deeply in chapter 4.

Eights need a lot of stimulation. They are constantly looking to fulfill their desires and are insatiable until they do.

For most Eights, they passionately pursue life and seek to live it to the fullest. Eights might be the type that is most aware of their own wants and desires, and the type that has the most resources to pursue those things. Eight wing sevens are even more prone to indulge in pleasures–we'll talk about wings in chapter 2.

If most people's average intensity levels are a 50 on a scale of 1-100, Eights average level is probably an 80-100.

This can lead to some of the best times you might ever have with a friend, but to also some of the nastiest fights you might ever encounter.

Eights truly don't know how to say "no." They will keep going, keep pushing, keep eating, or keep fighting until they burn out.

Scaling back this intensity will be key for Eights in learning to be around others, but we will talk more about that in later chapters.

With that baseline for all of us to move forward from, let's all pause for a second.

First, you may not totally resonate with every characteristic or my descriptions of them. That's okay. I am a bald, bearded, somewhat white, Seattle-living male. We might have a lot of differences.

But, I hope these descriptions at least give you a starting point or stir reflection in you. That's the whole point of this thing anyway.

Second, you probably still do not know what it fully means to be an Eight.

If you leave this book right now and go out into the world with these basics, you will cause more harm than understanding to the Eights around you.

One of the worst possible things you can do to your Eights is misunderstand them.

Lucky for you all, most Enneagram book's explorations of Eights end here. Not us, we got seven more chapters baby.

So, keep reading.

CHAPTER TWO

VARI8TIONS

You may be thinking, "I don't fit the Eight in some areas, I must not be an Eight!"

Welcome to the club. Nobody really matches every definition. We are all individuals with our own unique stories and personalities.

When I first began studying the Enneagram Eight, I often didn't relate to many of the descriptions. I felt they were slightly off, misguided, or just flat out wrong.

However, as I explored the different variations of the Eight and listened to stories from actual Eights, I related more to the type.

If you look up the descriptions of a Sexual dominant, Self-Preservation repressed, Eight wing Seven, you might see a photo of me and my bald head staring back at you. It's a beautiful photo, if I may say so.

If you don't know the Enneagram well, most of how I just described myself probably makes no sense to you. That's okay, I'll explain below.

Let's talk about the different wings and subtypes that add color and diversity to the Eight.

Wings

Although I wish this chapter were about all the different types of chicken wings–medium bone-in are the best–we are unfortunately talking about something less spicy and diarrhea-inducing.

In the Enneagram, there is a theory that you take on attributes from the types adjacent to your number.

For the Eight, our two wings are the Seven and the Nine. The wing number adds some of their basic desires, motivations, and weaknesses to our base number.

Most people have one dominant wing with access to the other wing in specific situations and scenarios. Some even have different wings depending on the context or social group they are currently in.

Some Enneagram theorists believe you have access to both wings at all times and in all situations. However, they're wrong and stupid. In my (correct) opinion, you only have access to one wing with the other wing showing up situationally.

For me, I have found that I am an Eight wing Seven most of the time. In my social circles and workplaces, you will see my Eight wing Seven very clearly. But, in my own family context back home, I resemble more of an Eight wing Nine.

If you've ever asked an Eight what their wing is, there's a good chance they told you they are an Eight wing Seven. It seems that Eight wing Sevens are far more common than Eight wing Nines.

Why is this you might ask?

There are probably many reasons for this, but I would propose that one of the main reasons is that the Eight wing Seven seems like the more fun and powerful wing. So, Eights normally identify more with that aspect of themselves.

As an Eight, would you rather have attributes from the "Enthusiast" or the "Peacemaker?"

The answer is quite easy if you are an Eight to your core. No shade to my lovely Nines out there, but the wing Seven fits much better with our desire to be strong and powerful adversaries. It's really hard to be a peacemaker when you're fighting people.

With all of that said, let's explore the two wings for the Eight.

Eight Wing Seven - The Maverick (Nonconformist)

The Eight wing Seven is the more animated of the two wings of the Eight.

Eight wing Sevens are more blunt, outgoing, aggressive, and reckless. They are also more impulsive, impatient, and action oriented of the two wings.

Since they take on some of the Seven attributes, they become the most independent type on the whole Enneagram as Sevens also value their independence. The Eight wing Seven probably needs very little of anything from anyone–at least on the surface. Underneath that independence, there's much more happening.

These Eights are business savvy and action oriented. They are more entrepreneurial than Eight wing Nines and are more confident and assertive. Eight wing Sevens are the people you want on your team to get things done and have original ideas.

They usually express their love for others by creating opportunities for them and pushing their boundaries. With the Seven's enthusiasm, they are the more lighthearted and humorous variation of the Eight.

However, the wing Seven also adds some blind spots and weak points.

Eight wing Sevens can lack compassion for how others are feeling. They tend to rush through things and get them done quickly and intensely. They are always in a "go go go" mode and can become frustrated with others' slower pace. Impulsivity is the Eight wing Sevens drug.

In work settings, Eight wing Sevens will make big promises and exaggerate what is possible to others. They will over promise and underdeliver since they are frequently doing too much. They can also prioritize what they want without considering others' wants and needs.

These types might also spend more money on unhealthy indulgences and experiences than the other Eight types. They couple the Eight's lust with the Seven's gluttony to make a relentless indulger.

Speaking from experience, almost all of my money goes towards food and fun.

Spending $150 on a new pair of shoes? No chance.

Spending $150 on a weekend of cheesesteaks and funnel cake at a theme park? Count me in.

Eight wing Sevens are truly some of the most passionate, energetic, driven, and larger-than-life beings on the planet.

If you want to learn more about what the wing Seven adds to your Eight persona, I recommend reading up on the wonderful, fanciful, and hopeful Enneagram Seven.

Eight Wing Nine - The Diplomat

The Eight wing Nine is the more compassionate of the two wings of the Eight.

They are more steady, measured, and approachable than the Eight wing Seven. These types are quietly powerful, kindhearted, private, and watchful. These Eights tend to hide their power and want others to underestimate them.

In some ways, the Eight wing Nine is a paradox. They feel torn between wanting to be confrontational (Eight-like) and wanting to keep the peace (Nine-like). This Enneagram type can struggle to figure out what to do with their intense anger while also trying to remain agreeable with others.

In the workplace, these Eights are more willing to work with and for others. They can be more accommodating and withdrawing to avoid tension. Although still primarily a fighter type, these types tend to flee more when faced with anxiety or fear.

In terms of added blind spots, the Eight wing Nine tends to be less aggressive and confrontational than the Eight wing Seven but can have an unpredictable temper. In some ways, the Eight wing Nine is far more likely to erupt with anger since they push their anger down more than the Eight wing Seven.

On their worst days, these types can be intimidating to others due to their quiet, cold anger. Partners and close friends are often unsure of when the Eight wing Nine's temper will explode, so they end up walking on eggshells around them. These Eights are also less willing to express how they feel. However, they can also become very stubborn and dig in their heels on the things they truly want like Enneagram Nines tend to do.

If you want to learn more about what the wing Nine adds to your Eight persona, I recommend reading up on the kind-hearted, peaceful, and easygoing Enneagram Nine.

Eight wing Sevens and Eight wing Nines share much in common. They are both Eights, after all.

However, the Eight wing Seven will be more passionate whereas the Eight wing Nine will be more idealistic. Eight wing Sevens will value freedom over peace while Eight wing Nines will value peace over freedom.

In some ways, you can tell the difference between the two wings by looking at their childhood development and how that plays out in their lives as adults.

Did they learn to pursue independence, experiences, and free will in order to find safety? They are probably an Eight wing Seven.

Did they learn to take on the role of guardian, protector, and peace maker at an early age in order to fit in? They are probably an Eight wing Nine.

As we mentioned before, you have access to both wings. It's important to discover which wing shows up more prominently and in what ways. If you can discover that, you have added another tool to your toolbelt to help you grow into a healthier person.

And no, you can't be an Eight wing Eight. I don't care how badass you think you are.

Subtypes

Beyond the wings, it is important to spend some time covering the subtypes of the Eight.

Again, if you are interested in finding out all about what an Enneagram subtype is, there are books in the references section to learn more from.

But, we simply do not have time to cover every single thing about the Enneagram if we want to fully cover the Eights–and we are not even fully covering the Eights.

In short, the "subtypes" are basic strategies used to survive the perceived threats of the world.

The subtypes focus on how these basic strategies show up in day-to-day life. With the Enneagram, each subtype is layered by the specific Enneagram number's emotional energy–in our case, the Eight's lust.

There are 3 basic subtypes: Self-Preservation, Social, and Sexual (one on one).

Self-Preservation	Social	Sexual (One on One)
These types survived by responding to the perceived threats and needs of their physical well-being	These types survived by creating social structures within communities and relying upon them	These types survived by looking to their primary relationships for security and comfort

In each Enneagram number, one of these subtypes is the countertype.

This is the type that has attributes that may make them appear different from the other numbers in their Enneagram because of how their subtype changes their type.

For instance, Social Eights often struggle to initially identify with the Eight since they are the countertype within the Eight. The Social subtype coupled with the Eight may make them appear different from most other Eights.

It might be helpful to illustrate subtypes with the scene of a house party.

The Self-Preservation type walks into a party with their partner and immediately realizes how warm or cold the room is. They might scan to see if there is ample refreshments and food available. While doing this, they will admire the decor of the house and think about what the decor says about the host. Finally, the Self-Preservation type might be the first to leave the party with their partner because they know exactly when their physical and social energy is used up.

The Social type walks into the party and immediately notices the group congregating near the fireplace. They are looking to see what different groups of people are at the party and who they might most fit in with. Before long, the Social type will ingratiate themselves into their chosen group and partake in whatever games, conversations, or jokes the group is engaged in. The Social type will leave the party once their group breaks up and only little pockets of people are left.

The Sexual type walks into the party and immediately scans the room for the most interesting person in the room or for someone they can enter into a deep conversation with. Although they see the group congregating by the fireplace, they might try and steal away someone from that group to engage them in a more intimate conversation. The Sexual type might end up talking with this person the whole night or find someone new after that conversation loses its zest. The Sexual type will be the last to leave the party and they might not be leaving the party alone either.

Each person has one dominant subtype, one neutral subtype, and one repressed subtype.

It is super important to figure out which subtype you are dominant in as well as which subtype you are repressed in. This will help you understand your Enneagram number on a deeper level.

For the Eight, we will dive into each of these three subtypes and how they vary from one another. We'll also discuss what it looks like to be dominant and repressed in a subtype.

Self-Preservation Eight - The Survivalist

Although this Eight is known as "the Survivalist," Enneagram expert Beatrice Chestnut says that the key word for this subtype is "satisfaction."

Self-Preservation (SP) Eights focus on their needs for material survival and security. These needs generally include food, family relationships, home life, and physical well-being.

SP Eights are survivors and pillars of strength in their lives as they take the role of guardian, father, or mother figure.

In this subtype, Eights will pursue the things they need to survive in direct, powerful, and passionate ways.

This might look like an Eight pursuing their career ambitions in order to set up themselves and their future generations financially. It might also look like the Eight making their partner change their plans on a vacation so they can indulge in a food or drink delicacy.

These Eights might also be interested in money as power more than the other Eights. They can become protective over their homes and belongings. It's not uncommon for SP Eights to constantly check their finances. With money, they can become bullies and thieves while they justify their shady expenditures.

Stressed SP Eights may even squirrel away possessions and materials with the mindset of "What's mine is mine and what's yours is yours."

However, don't let this reality fool you into thinking SP Eights are exclusively hoarders. They can be extremely generous with their money. It just depends on where they are at. If a SP Eight is feeling healthy and loving, they will be the most generous of all the Eight types.

SP Eights are often more practical minded and resourceful than the other Eights. These Eights are the ones you would want to take with you into uncertain environments since they excel at finding material support to survive. They also might be the best dressed of all of the Eights due to their attention and appreciation of physical presentation.

Because of their aggressive pursuit to take care of their own needs, this Eight can come across as the most selfish of all the Eights. They will appear intolerant to the needs of those around them as they pursue satisfying their own needs. These Eights can be very territorial and will secure the perimeter of their lives.

SP Eights can also come across as the most guarded and least emotionally sharing out of all the Eights. These Eights keep their cards close to their chest. They generally appear more aggressive than the Social Eight but also much less charismatic and rebellious than the Sexual Eight.

If you are repressed in the Self-Preservation subtype, you might be prone to not taking care of yourself and your material world. This might look like neglecting physical health and the environment you live in. Repressed SP types might wear all of their emotions on their sleeve and overshare compared to how the SP dominant types are more guarded.

Being a repressed SP type myself, I can tell you that repressed SP types need to learn how to take care of themselves. Emotionally, physically, or even just in the care of your home, repressed SP types need to find ways to become more balanced in these areas.

Overall, SP Eights are the more reserved, financially stable, and stylish type of the Eights.

Social Eight - The Group Leader

Known as the "Group Leader" or "Gang Leader," this Eight's key word is "solidarity."

Social (SO) Eights focus on finding groups or causes to establish security for themselves. These Eights overcome their feelings of helplessness by leading the charge in their groups.
The SO Eight is considered the countertype of the Eight. As an Eight, they want to rebel against social norms, yet as a SO Eight, they want to be loyal to groups and society. Because of this, social Eights often mistype as Sixes, Nines, or Twos.

These Eights are more loyal, outwardly mellow, overtly friendly, and helpful than the other Eights. Although still rebellious, they are more subtle in their rebellion than the other Eight types. They are more concerned with the injustice that happens to society and groups rather than individuals.

These types are super susceptible to betrayal (as all Eights are), but they can often feel the betrayal stronger than the other subtypes since they feel betrayal on the group level. Because of this, they can hold grudges longer than the other Eights.

Sensitive to injustice and unfair social norms, they are loyal and protective. These Eights shield those around them from harm, injustice, or abuse.

Even though this Eight comes across softer, they still struggle with tending to their own needs. SO Eights frequently get so caught up in pursuing justice for groups that they themselves get neglected.

If you are a repressed Social type, then you might find that you are fairly antagonistic towards groups and organizations. These repressed types might show up as one of the more rebellious Eight types as they don't find belonging in any social group. It will be healthy for repressed SO types to learn to trust larger groups and find belonging in some of them–maybe even just one.

SO Eights are the most agreeable, friendly, and accommodating of the Eights.

Sexual Eight - The Commander

This Eight type is known as "the Commander" with their key word being "possession."

The Sexual (SX) Eight might be the most intense personality type of the whole Enneagram. This version of the Eight is more emotionally intense and reactive than the other Eights.

SX Eights are the most charismatic, alluring, and captivating of all of the Eights.

With their partners or close friends, this Eight usually struggles with trying to control them. This control is rooted in the SX Eight finding security in their close relationships and wanting to make sure they don't lose them. They can be way more demanding of others and their time.

This possessiveness can also come out in the SX Eight's desire to dominate a room through their charisma. These Eights can quickly become the energy center of a gathering. In other words, these Eights believe that, "The party doesn't start until I arrive."

At their worst, SX Eights can try and mold others into what they need them to be. They will dominate their partner and become extremely jealous and possessive.

Outside of the possessive side of the SX Eight, they might be the most rebellious type on the whole Enneagram. SX Eights see society as a place to be challenged and even broken if necessary. These Eights are the most willing to provoke and disrupt others.

This type, even more than the other Eight types, likes to be seen as bad. They do not feel guilt over most of the rebellious things they do. They want to stand apart from the social norms around them.

Don't let this desire to "be bad" make you think SX are malicious. They have big hearts and want to do good for others. They just don't care to conform to society's values and virtues unless they align with their own.

The Eight's desire for intensity is most clearly seen in this subtype as they are constantly seeking out their next powerful encounter or experience. These Eights are the most drawn to other's energy out of all of the Eights.

They want to play a vital role in the lives of their loved ones and their organizations. They seek out risky adventures and are voracious in their pursuit of sex and pleasure. SX Eights are always chasing after energy. These Eights are the most magnetic and seductive of the subtypes.

SX Eights feel things very deeply which can cause a problem for those around them if their needs are not met. Because of their intensity, these Eights can often be mistaken for sexual Fours since they are the most emotional of all the Eights.

If you are a repressed Sexual type, you might discover that you do not find much safety in your close relationships. Although all humans do find safety in the intimacy of their peers, repressed SX types often look to their own home environments or groups to find those. It is super important if you are repressed SX that you find people you can trust and rely upon–as that is important for all Eights as well.

Overall, SX Eights are the more intense, emotional, and rebellious type of the Eights.

Female Eights

No, women are not variants of the Eight.

However, in a male-dominated world, these descriptions of the Eight might be somewhat insufficient for female Eights.

Again, I am writing this book through the lens of my own life experiences as a man. Although I have talked with many female Eights to prepare for this book, it is important to dedicate a section to fully express the social differences between male and female Eights.

Nigerian-British author Jo Saxton is a great example of a female Eight. When she was finding out her Enneagram type, she said, "just find the one where you get called all the names as a woman." Not surprisingly, many female Eights have similar experiences to this.

Since the Eight embodies a very traditionally masculine archetype, it makes it hard for female Eights to figure out their inner life in relation to their outer expression. Since Western society has largely assigned strength, confidence, and courage to masculinity, it makes it tricky for female Eights to figure out what that expression might look like in themselves.

In other words, to be a female Eight is to be somewhat sneaky and covert with power.

Female Eights are diplomats. They know when to harness the power and leadership that most Eights are natural to.

To quote my good female Eight friend Sabrina Strom, who quotes Theodore Roosevelt, being a female Eight is "speaking softly and carrying a big stick." It is the Machiavellian concept of being "sly as a fox and powerful as a lion."

Whereas male Eights are more likely to identify with the Eight wing Seven, female Eights are more likely to identify as Eight wing Nine due to societal pressures and expectations. Obviously, as powerful women become more commonplace in society, more female Eight Wing Sevens will arise.

Female Eights usually can benefit in ways that male Eights may not, especially in their access to the softer sides of their inner world. They are often in more physically comforting friendships and relationships. Since Eights (secretly) crave tenderness and the safety of physical touch, women naturally have more access to this in their different relationships since it is more socially acceptable.

On the other side of the coin, female Eights are frequently enraged at the societal expectations placed upon them to be more tender and softer. Their anger can fester as they see society view women as weak.

They are often viewed as "intimidating" in their social circles and workplaces. However, most female Eights have learned how to manage their anger in situations where male Eights don't have to. This is an injustice that male Eights don't have to deal with.

In the workplace, these Eight traits get men promotions and women scoldings. Men act in accordance with the Eight personality and get called "great leaders." Women act in accordance with the Eight personality and get called "bitches." Female Eight leaders are generally viewed more as a loud annoyance than a blessing to the team. They often get called "too much" and "domineering."

Although all Eights feel the need to censor themselves, female Eights especially have to censor themselves. Female Eights will have to change their style, their hair, and even their posture to try to come off less intimidating in the workplace. Unfortunately for most female Eights, even these efforts do not succeed in changing the perception of them.

Needless to say, it is much more difficult to be a female Eight in our society than a male Eight.

Some of my female Eight friends have said that it is extremely hard to be healthy and find other healthy female Eights. There is such a tension between wanting to go against those above and around you and yet constantly feeling like the system (men) are lording over you. Because of this, there are very few places for female Eights to just be themselves and grow in who they are.

If you are reading this and you identify as a female Eight, I am so glad you exist.

We need you in our world. Your strength, power, vision, and courage are so needed. As society continues to progress and make space for strong female leaders like yourselves, I hope you can find places and spaces to use your gifts now.

Overall, there are many ways to be an Eight. If you are struggling to find your place in the Eight, that's okay.

Maybe you're just not an Eight. Maybe you're a counterphobic Six, which is the most common mistype for Eights.

However, if you are an Eight and you do resonate with many of the basics, then it will be helpful for you to find your wings and subtype. These added layers of the Enneagram can bring more areas of understanding and growth to you as a person.

If you're lost, just ask your friends what they think.

I know, it's a crazy fucking idea to allow others to tell you about yourself. But trust me, they might know you and see you more clearly than you do in certain areas.

Just maybe.

CHAPTER THREE

THE ORIGIN STORY

Like most superheroes–and all Enneagram types–the Eight's origin story is key to understanding their current reality.

From their childhood, the Eight was born.

Some Enneagram experts argue that you are born as your type. Although there's some merit to this, I believe your type is formed through your childhood experiences.

If you want to believe that our personalities are fixed at birth, you can go study astrology–no shade to my astrologers out there, but I mean... c'mon. Y'all know personality is more complex than star arrangements at birth.

For all of us, we have certain personalities as kids. Yet, we are also moldable as children. We might lean towards certain personality traits naturally, but we also grow into others due to our experiences.

One theory I have, although completely unproven, is that your stress number on the Enneagram is the number you most relate to in your childhood self.

For instance, the stress number for Eights is the Five. As an Eight, I perceive my childhood self as a shy, fearful, quiet, introverted, and observing kid. However, due to some key life experiences, I realized I could no longer stay that way if I wanted to survive in this world. So, I shed those traits and developed strength, courage, action, and extroversion. I compensated for my weaknesses and became an Eight.

Now, this doesn't mean that my childhood self was a Five. Rather, it simply means that when I think of my childhood self, I perceive him as a Five. In times of stress, I revert back to my childhood self and take on Five qualities.

In more extreme cases of this, psychologists call this "regression." This is when an adult literally starts to act like a child again.

On a smaller scale, we take on attributes of our childhood selves when we are stressed. Since an Eight acts like a Five when they are stressed, this may be what their childhood self was like.

That's just a theory. If it's helpful, run with it. If it's not, then you can email me and tell me how fucking stupid I am.

Either way, your childhood matters.

The Eight Childhood

It might be hard for you to believe, but your childhood shaped you into the person you are today.

There are memories (conscious and unconscious) that drive your current adult behaviors.

From wounds to narratives to pivotal events to watching your caretakers interact to even your genetics, your personality is the sum of all those factors.

Enneagram expert Beatrice Chestnut observed that Eights were usually the youngest and smallest child in a family. Survival depended on denying the fact that they were small.

I have observed, however, that Eights are also often the oldest child in the family. In this case, they were handed responsibility at too young an age.

Obviously, you can be the youngest, oldest, middle, or even an only child and be an Eight. What's most important is the narratives that you took with you from childhood.

Regardless of what position you were in your family, Eight's learned to take on responsibility and simultaneously rebel in their youth. Much of the Eight's rebellion can be traced back to their relationships with the authority figures in their home growing up.

Eights learned to not expect anything from authority figures at a young age. They learned they couldn't truly depend on them. So, the Eight became their own authority figure.

For me, my Eight origin story starts with a Sicilian family.

I am the youngest child in my family.

My father is one of the most typical Phobic Six wing Fives you can ever meet. My mother, to me, is one of the most typical Enneagram Twos. In my research of the Eight, I have found that this is a common Enneagram parent pairing that leads to an Eight child, at least for male Eights.

My older brother is a classic Enneagram One—which I have also observed that Eights often have Enneagram One authority figures in their lives growing up. As for my older sister, she is an Enneagram Three, but she also has a lot of Eight in her. I was younger than both of them by a few years, which led to an interesting dynamic with the rest of the family.

At a young age, I slowly learned to handle myself. Through competing with my older siblings in sports, enduring hardships with my parents going through difficult financial times, and learning from the mistakes of my older siblings, I was always a few steps ahead of the kids my age.

I was groomed to be wiser, stronger, and more mature than my peers.

My siblings viewed me as the golden child of my parents, but I frequently felt like an outsider looking into the happenings of my family.

As the youngest child, you are usually watching the family affairs happen. You are too young to have any say, too small to make any real impact, and too innocent to be included in the real-life shit that happens. However, as most kids do, I still noticed all that was happening in our family.

This powerlessness I felt as a child led me to develop my "Eight" outside of the family. I became the ringleader of my friend groups, the leader of my sports teams, and even began to teach myself school after 4th grade–I was homeschooled until 7th grade but due to my parents barely graduating High School in the 80's, they couldn't really help me beyond 4th grade.

Around my middle school years, my Eightness started to come into form. It all happened in a few different memories.

Memories that changed everything for me. Memories that made me an adult. Memories that made me an Eight

Your story might look different than mine. You might have different parental dynamics and sibling realities. Your story might have more trauma or abuse than mine. Many Eights do.

The point is to discover what's behind your actions and struggles. The "why" is what we're getting at, but that "why" is normally buried in childhood memories and narratives.

For Eights, one of the biggest things is the loss of innocence in childhood. Our next section will dive into what happened.

The Switch

Most Eights that have done self-reflection or story work will tell you that there was a specific period where they switched from being a child to becoming an adult.

A moment in time when everything changed. When they left childhood behind. When they suddenly grew into their bodies and personality. When they became a strong, confident, and courageous adult.

We will call this moment or period "The Switch." I borrowed this language from Sleeping at Last's song "Eight" that is based on the Enneagram Eight.

For Eights, "The Switch" often happened abruptly.

One moment, they were children full of wonder, innocence, and optimism. The next moment, they were adults full of responsibility, determination, and strength.

"The Switch" is usually centered around memories of helplessness, weakness, or powerlessness. It was a childhood moment or moments where their backs were against the wall. It was a childhood experience where their fear and sadness finally gave way to anger and vengeance.

It was a moment where Eights asked themselves, "How did this happen? How could I have been duped? How could I have allowed this to happen to me? I should have known better. I should have known that I was alone in this dangerous world. I should have not let this happen to me."

It is this side of their stories that Eights hate. They believe they got hurt because of their neediness. They got abused because of their weakness. They got humiliated because of their helplessness.

Eights are often criticized for shaming others' sensitivity and weakness. But, this is simply a projection of their own self-contempt.

Eights experience a lot of shame for their memories and moments of helplessness in childhood. Many Eights might even start to believe that they betrayed themselves as children by not being prepared for the danger life threw at them. In an Eight's mind, they allowed their own vulnerable self to be wounded.

As I have talked to many Eights, "The Switch" memory is frequently visceral. They can remember it in their bodies. They can feel the event coursing through their veins. Some even recall the moment that fear turned into anger in a split second.

For some, "The Switch" was a specific moment in time where everything changed.

For others, "The Switch" was not a singular moment but a period of time when their life changed.

For many, "The Switch" started with some early memories of helplessness and culminated in one final moment that ended all hope of them being protected by anyone other than themselves.

Oftentimes, "The Switch" starts at a younger age (9 years old in my case) and culminates in one final moment in their later years (17 in my case). Some might point to their younger moment as "The Switch," while others will point to their older moment as "The Switch."

If you are unsure of when this happened, I normally ask Eights this question to try and pinpoint the time period: "When you picture your childhood self, how old are you?"

For most people, the age of their childhood self or the oldest age of what they perceive to be their child-self is around the time "The Switch" happened.

Ultimately, it's super important when exactly it happened but rather what changed in you. It's important to pinpoint what changed when you told yourself, "I will never let this happen again."

For my friend Brianna–not her real name, none of these names are real–the start of her "Switch" happened when she was twelve.

It was a normal afternoon after school.

Brianna and her sister, Abbey, were upstairs while her sister was getting ready to host one of her high school friends.

Brianna started to talk with Abbey about her day at school, her thoughts on the book she was reading, and her opinions on the newest season of America's Next Top Model. It seems as if the excess of Briana's excitement began to agitate Abbey. So, Abbey began to ignore her.

Being a young 12-year-old, Brianna continued to press, living out her excitement in the seemingly safe environment of her sister's bedroom. Somewhere in between breaths, Abbey lashed out. She yelled at Brianna, striking a simultaneously exhaustive and passionate attack. Her sister's harshness confused Brianna and wounded her.

Somewhere in a long monologue of energized hate, Abbey spat, "You are horrible, Brianna. Look at you cry. You're just like dad. No wonder no one likes you–no wonder no boys like you."

Brianna had not even noticed the tears that were streaming down her face.

With that, Abbey left Brianna and went downstairs. Briana then wept and wailed for what felt like an eternity. It felt like she had to cry, and yet she knew she was risking her safety with each tear that dropped. Brianna knew that if her mom heard her, she would experience another berating.

Quickly, Brianna walked out of the room, turned the corner into the shared bathroom, and looked at herself in the mirror.

There she was: a chubby, 12-year-old facing her reflection in the mirror with contempt—hating her puffy face and tear-stained t-shirt.

Briana proceeded to place her hands down on the counter, lean in close, and say, "I don't cry. I do not cry."

She must have repeated it ten times over, for in that moment she chose to abandon her tender self for the sake of her protection and survival. Brianna started the journey of walking away from her soft self so that she could survive the next six years in that home.

For Brianna, these early moments of her "Switch" showed her the pathway to safety. She had to deny weakness. To not show her vulnerabilities. To shut off her fragile side. To tell her tears to go suck it.

For me, the start of "The Switch" happened over the course of a few years from ages 9-13. I have some vivid memories from this time, a lot of them related to the feelings surrounding "The Switch."

I can remember being about 9 years old and playing my older brother in Madden (which is a football videogame for you non-nerds).

My older cousin was over and us three would often hangout, even though I was 5 years younger than both of them.

As you can imagine, I got my ass whooped in Madden. But, just losing the game wasn't enough for the older kids. It's never enough for the older siblings. They had to rub my face in my defeat.

As any normal 9-year-old child would do, I burst into tears and ran into the nearby bathroom to escape their harassment. But, that wasn't enough for them either. They needed more of my humiliation. They were absolutely delighted in what was happening.

They found a screwdriver and worked on unlocking the door. I was sitting on the toilet trying to compose myself–I knew my mom and dad weren't coming to help–and heard them rustling outside with the lock.

I started to panic. I was trapped. I was afraid. My body was convulsing with fear and anxiety.

It was at this moment that I experienced the first rumblings of my "Switch."
Suddenly, without even thinking about it, my body turned some of that roaring panic into rage. I felt the fear leave my brain and a rush of adrenaline and anger flow through my head to my fists.

I was ready to fight back.

As they opened the door, I wiped my tears, stood up, and screamed at them "I HATE YOU! GO AWAY!"

To my surprise, they left me alone. Sitting in that bathroom, I marveled at my fists and the power they held.

I had discovered a new ability. This ability that told me I can turn my fear into fight, my retreat into rage, and my sobbing into smashing.

Luckily for all those around me (including myself), I didn't start immediately beating up every little kid that looked at me the wrong way on the bus. It still took some time for "The Switch" to fully take root in my life. The full culmination of "The Switch" didn't happen until I was 17.

For all of us Eights, we need to explore these memories. These are crucial to our healing and growth as Eights. So much of our pain is tied to these moments. So much of our current reality can be traced back to these moments.

We lost a lot when "The Switch" happened. Lost our childhood. Lost our sense of safety. Lost our trust in the world.
Most importantly, we lost our innocence and ability to be nurtured.

Innocence and Nurture

If you've been in the Enneagram scene a while, you would have heard about the Eight needing to rediscover their innocence.

But, what does that even mean? Are you telling me that I need to be a gullible, naive, little kid again? Why the hell would I do that?

When most people find out that their friend is an Eight, they sometimes (with good intentions) try and point out the Eight's tender side.

Enneagram experts have perpetuated this idea that Eights are big and angry on the outside and soft as a marshmallow on the inside. Those that know the Enneagram know that Eights have this vulnerable and innocent self underneath the surface, so they speak tenderly to Eights.

This often doesn't work. If anything, it might piss off the Eight. It sure as hell pisses me off.

Well, at least it used to piss me off. I am writing a book about the Eight, right? I finally figured this shit out–Okay, who am I kidding? It still pisses me off.

This view of the Eight lacks nuance. It lacks the depth of why Eights are angry. It lacks the understanding of that tender internal self. Most of the time, tenderness gets weaponized against an Eight when they are acting strong.

If you are friends with an Eight, do not use their soft sides to shut down their strong sides. It won't work. You need to make room for both.

Even though people use it against us, there is still something of value in recapturing our innocence as Eights. Most lost their innocence when "The Switch" happened.

It was a loss of childhood. A loss of being able to depend on those older than them. Unspeakable, unimaginable, inconsolable loss.

Eights often report abuse or neglect in childhood. In Donald Trump's case (a classic Enneagram Eight), it's been reported that his dad emotionally abused him. He would publicly belittle him and humiliate him to toughen up his son.

For some Eights who suffered emotional abuse and not physical abuse, there's a part of them where they actually wished they were hit rather than mocked and belittled. In their minds, they would have rather endured the physical abuse than the emotional humiliation.

As a child, Eights had to take matters into their own hands to get their needs met. They had to develop a belief that they were strong and even invincible. They had to believe they were invulnerable.

Much of the pain in an Eight's internal world is wrapped around these memories. Whether they are conscious of it or not, Eights are desperately wanting to be protected, nurtured, and taken care of.

Simultaneously, Eights are also disgusted by super nurturing people. It makes us sick to see adults babied and nurtured like children. It's really a horrible paradox we've found ourselves in.

The reason for this is that Eights lost connection to the nurturing parent–usually the mother, but not always–when they were kids.

In many Eights I've spoken with, they often had Enneagram Two mothers–and Enneagram Six fathers–who used their care and nurture towards them in manipulative fashions. For some, it felt like the nurture came from a place of manipulation. For others, their nurturing parent pretended to be caring for their Eight child when they both knew that the child was really taking care of their parent.

Mom wanted to care for us to fulfil her own needs. We couldn't accept it.

This inevitably leads to the painful reality of Eights rejecting nurture entirely.

In object relations theory (not enough time to get into all of it, you can google it) Eights are in the rejection triad.

All babies need protection (normally the father figure) and nurture (normally the mother figure). For Eights, they learned to shut off their need for nurture. Instead, they overidentified with the protection side and became physical protection itself. This rejection of nurture plays a key role in the adult life of the Eight. "The Switch" is generally tied to this rejection.

We can see this rejection of nurture in the story of my friend Emerson.

For Emerson, his loss of nurture was on display when he was 16.

As he recounted the story to me, he had just had his heart broken by a girl from a youth group. He remembered coming home and seeing his mom sitting at the table on her computer. Emerson was in a full-blown, enraged fit of sadness.

Instead of going to his mom for comfort and consolation, he walked straight past her and headed outside. He unconsciously moved to one of the orange trees in the backyard near the wall.

Once he got there, he grabbed orange after orange and threw them as hard as he could against the wall. Again, and again, and again.

With rage and tears flowing, he continued to throw the oranges with his whole strength.

His mom ended up coming out to see if she could help. However, no matter how much she tried to comfort or talk to her son, he just kept throwing the oranges at the wall. The only thing that brought him a little comfort was the sound of the oranges when they hit the wall.

He could not be consoled. He could not be nurtured. He could not be cared for.

Many of us have stories like Emerson's.

Memories where we were going through a crisis moment and had nowhere to turn. Memories where we wished we had someone stronger, older, bigger, or braver that we trusted to handle things. Memories where there was no comfort to be found in those around us.

The only person we could turn to was ourselves.

I know this is true of my own story.

When I was 17, my loss of nurture and dependence on my parents culminated in one moment.

In high school, I was a starter on the varsity basketball team. This was a huge deal. My brother had been a starter before me and we had been training since we were 5 years old for moments like these.

Unfortunately, I hit a slump and got benched from the starting lineup.

For my 17-year-old self, this was devastating.

Like Emerson's story, I remember walking past my father sitting on our couch and heading outside after I got home from practice that day. In my family, we had experienced this before when my brother was benched by the same coach. That time, my dad made me go outside with him to rebound for my brother and comfort him while he practiced.

I was expecting the same reality for me. However, when I had been out on the court for a while, my dad still hadn't come out.

What could this be? Why wasn't he coming out to help me? Does he not know I'm out here?

I was doing all the necessary things for comfort after getting benched. I followed the script from my older brother in order to be cared for.

Wasn't this supposed to be a moment of triumphing over failure with my dad? Wasn't this supposed to be a moment where he told me everything was going to be okay, and he loved me? Wasn't this the moment where I could look at him and he would guide me out of this?

As the time ticked on, I became more enraged and despairing. With tears streaming down my face and anger coursing through my veins, I began to throw the ball at the backboard as hard as I could.

I thought, "Maybe if he could just hear that I was out here, he would come out like he did for my brother."

After a few minutes of this, he never did.

With the rage still exploding in me and the sadness bubbling in my throat, I threw the ball one last time against the backboard and kicked it over the wall.

I decided that from that point forward, I would depend on nobody to help me through these moments.

Not my dad, not my mom, not my siblings, not my friends, nobody. The only person you could rely on was yourself and that's who I would turn to.

The painful reality is that we lost our connection to nurture itself. In this way, we also lost our innocence at far too young an age.

This loss of innocence can lead to some Eights becoming fixated on childlike things. You will see Eights have collections of action figures and childhood tokens. They might also play certain childhood games or be drawn to pets and animals. These things frequently become fixations for Eights as they subconsciously try to relive their childhood that was lost.

In this loss, Eights need to learn to have compassion on their inner child. They need to learn to make space for that fragile, helpless kid. It might even be helpful to give a name to your inner child.

For me, I named my inner child "Coco" which was my childhood nickname.

In a particularly tough season for me, I spent a lot of time feeling like I was a scared, shy, and lonely kid again.

There was a part of me that wanted to shame that kid into toughening up and facing his fears. But, from my work with the Enneagram, I tried to learn how to be gracious to Coco. To see the good in him. To notice how amazing it was that Coco decided to survive in this way: by learning to face his fears and conquer his monsters.

It's honestly incredible that some children decide to become Eights when faced with their fears rather than caving to them. This is something to marvel at, not shame. Although these coping mechanisms might not be helpful anymore as adults, what a beautiful thing they were to help us survive childhood.

For you, maybe it's not naming your inner child but finding an image, metaphor, or memory that depicts your younger self. This could be a specific hobby you loved as a kid or a certain vacation or trip your family went on. It could be a moment of fun with your friends or when you discovered something new that blew your mind. It could be a pivotal moment of change or hurt. It could be a favorite toy or stuffed animal that was always with you as a kid. Literally, anything that resonates with how you picture your younger self.

Spend time in that image. Befriend that story. Sit in that memory with trusted friends and allies. Wade into the sadness of that moment. Explore those long-lost fears and anxieties. Those fears are still here even if you are unaware of them.

We'll talk more about engaging with our younger selves in our last chapter.

Triangulating Our Childhood

No, this isn't about actual triangles or some weird form of Geometry.

This section is about the psychological term from family therapy called "Triangulation."

Some psychologists argue that there are good versions of triangulation, but we will be focusing on the negative effects of destabilizing triangulation.

Negative triangulation shows up in a family when two people avoid dealing with their current problem and bring a third person into it.

For instance, if your mom and dad have conflict but do not want to deal with it directly, one of them might go vent to their child about their issue. This is a triangle because the conflict should stay between the two at the top, but they bring in a third party, therefore making it a triangle.

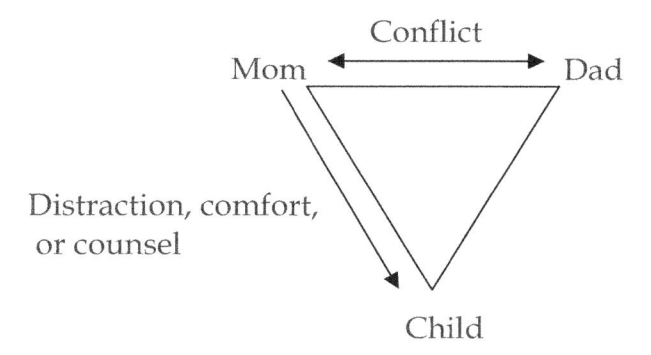

```
                    Conflict
            Mom ←─────────→ Dad
               \           /
                \         /
 Distraction, comfort,   /
    or counsel  \       /
                 \     /
                  \   /
                   ↓ ↓
                  Child
```

To illustrate this, I will tell you about an example from my own life.

When I was about 13 years old, I can remember my parents going through a rough time in their relationship.

My dad was out of work and struggling with depression, and my mom was having to work extra hours to make ends meet. Because of this, tension arose in their interpersonal dynamics.

Oftentimes, they would get in loud fights in their room upstairs. This is normally not a big deal. We are a culturally Sicilian family so passionate yelling isn't always a big deal.

However, these fights felt different. I can remember many times sitting downstairs and stressfully listening to their fights.

After their fights, my mom would be the first to come back downstairs. She would often come directly to where I was playing video games or watching TV. She would wipe the tears from her eyes, sit down next to me, smile, and ask "how was your day at school, Honey?"

As a young teenager, I noticed the situation at hand. Subconsciously, I felt like I needed to comfort Mom. I needed to cheer her up. I needed to make things better for her. So, I told her that, "School was great."

I felt like I couldn't add my problems onto my parents' lives. I also felt special since my mom was coming to me to cheer her up. She didn't go to my other siblings. She didn't go to my father. She chose me.

However, I never felt like I could share what was really going on. I had to put my needs on the backburner to care for the needs of my parents. I had to take on the responsibility of making sure I didn't cause any more problems for my parents.

This is the reality of triangulation.

Instead of the parents dealing with their issues with one another, they will usually pick a special child to distract them or comfort them.

However, as you can see in my own story, this teaches children many things about what kinds of emotions are allowed and what kind of role the child must play in their parent-child dynamic.

For Eights, our childhood triangles often pushed us into adult-like roles. Whether the triangle taught you to be strong, to be funny, to be mature, to be happy, or to be in control, we all learned things from these unhealthy dynamics.

Usually, we subconsciously learned these things. This means that you might not even be aware of what you learned. But, I'm sure these narratives are showing up in your actions and thought patterns.

One of the hardest things about triangulation is that it can also create a defense mechanism in the child. You will become protective of that parent. You will excuse their behavior. You might even start to think that you were old enough or mature enough to comfort your adult parents. This is the trap of triangulation.

I know you might think that your parents were exempt from triangulation with you. I am sure your parents are great people. I am not here to shit on your parents. But, I would argue that almost all parents do this. It is simply humanity and how we exist. If you don't see it at first, look a little deeper.

It took me a while to recognize my own triangulation. I love my parents, and still do even with all the stories you will see in this book. They are human beings, with their own stories of hurt and trauma, doing their best to survive and love in this world.

Triangulation just happens. It's normal. It's human.

Admitting your parents weren't perfect isn't dishonoring them. If anything, it is honoring to see them for all that they are and still love them.

For others, I'm sure you didn't even hesitate to find these triangles. Maybe your parents actually were shitheads.

Regardless, all I'm saying is that admitting your triangles doesn't mean your parents are terrible people. Obviously, they still could be. But, the triangles aren't the reason for that.

For whoever is reading this book, it will be important for you to identify the triangles in your family of origin.

Did your dad or mom elevate you to an adult role by looking to you for counsel, comfort, or distraction? What internal narratives did you learn about yourself from this triangle? Was it not your mom or dad but some other authority figure in your life that brought you into a triangle?

No matter where your triangles lie, you have them. Find them.

Denying Our Tears

There's a deep sorrow buried far inside the Eight. An immense sadness. A huge well of grief.

As we have discussed before, Eights had to grow up way too quickly. As adults, there is frequently a deep, heavy, fathomless sadness that resides in the Eight.

Many Eights, whether they are aware of it or not, are terrified that if they start crying, they will never stop. I know it was my fear as I first entered therapy, and I've heard countless stories of fellow Eights who feared the same thing.

There's a part of this, like in Brianna's story above, where Eights learned that crying is a sign of weakness. We learned to be responsible, which left no room for tears and weakness.

Usually, Eights heard phrases like "you are so strong" or "you are so steady" which reinforced the idea that we couldn't let our guard down. Eights created strength to mask their sadness.

Psychologist Dr. Dan Allender has said "these strengths were the thing we relied on when we faced tragedy". They helped us make it through childhood.

However, Dr. Allender says that you also start to develop a love-hate relationship with your strengths. You hate them because it brings you back to your childhood and reminds you of what you had to go through. But, you also love them because they helped you survive childhood.

The beautiful strategies that your child-self used to survive have now become maladaptive strategies for you as an adult.

The very things that helped you survive childhood might now be slowly killing you in adulthood.

One part of the Eight's journey is to rediscover these softer, sadder, and weaker sides of themselves. Most Eight's tender heart will come out with weak and vulnerable things. For many Eights, it often comes out with animals or children.

I can think of no better example of this than my grandpa, Nanu.

Nanu was raised by Sicilian immigrants in the steel town of Johnstown, Pennsylvania.

He lived a rough and hard life. His mom died when he was still a boy and his dad was distant, abusive, and a serial womanizer. Because of this, he developed a strong, independent, and tough exterior.

In other words, Nanu is an Eight.

He ended up in the union and fought for workers' rights. He took on the big corporations in his steel town and made sure the little guy got treated fairly. However, he often didn't know how to set aside his protective and aggressive demeanor when he left the union.

My own father (a Six) can remember the toughness and roughness with which Nanu treated him in his childhood. He challenged him constantly. He yelled at him to make a difference in his life. He told him to get to work and that he could "sleep when he was dead." Needless to say, he was a tough father to my dad.

Of course, Nanu had good intentions. He was trying to prepare my dad for what he thought was a dangerous world. He figured he was doing my dad a favor by not going easy on him. But, he obviously went too far.

Without going into all the specifics of my dad's childhood, something changed when me and my siblings were born. My dad noticed a distinct change in the demeanor and personality of Nanu when he became a grandfather.

Nanu, now without the pressure of preparing his kids for adulthood, turned into a loving and tender grandpa. He would roll on the ground and play with us grandkids. He would dance and sing with us. He would let us drive around on his golf cart and sneak us treats. He even adopted a dog in his later years and treated her like she was his princess.

Obviously, this was complicated for my own father to see. In some ways, he loved seeing how Nanu interacted with me and my siblings. In other ways, he wished that Nanu could have been more tender to him when he was a child.

My dad wished our Nanu's tender side had come out to play much sooner in his life. He thinks it might have made a world of a difference.

This story is generally the case with most Eights.

They can be rough and tough with their own kids and family, but somehow a tender sweetheart to their pets. They can be demanding and challenging of their own children, but gracious and loving to their grandchildren.

For Eights, it's so important that they spend time around vulnerable beings. Whether that's pets, children, or some tender hobby they enjoy, it's vital that Eights interact with things they don't perceive to be a threat to themselves.

As Eights, we cannot wait until it's too late to start this work. We cannot project our strength and toughness onto everyone and everything around us.

It will kill those around us. It will harm those around us. It will push those closest to us away from us.

We need to discover our tender sides again.

We will talk more about what this looks like in chapter 8.

It is vital for Eights to engage their story.

We all came from somewhere. We all suffered pains, heartaches, and losses. We all made it through these moments. We are all survivors.

These moments still speak to us. They still inform how we act, think, and feel.

You can try to kill the weeds of your behaviors in your life. It may even work for a period of time. It might make your life 10x better than how it was before.

But, if you want a true and long-lasting transformation, you have to take the time to slowly, delicately, and deeply pull out the roots of those weeds. Dive into the abyss of your story and discover where your current realities come from. Remove the false narratives and painful roots in order to get rid of your current behavioral weeds.

This is the work of the Eight: to dive into our origin stories, befriend our childhood-self, and discover the path of healing for our adult-self.

It is hard work, but it is rewarding work.

To close, I would like to share a journal entry from pages 49-50 of *The Inner Voice of Love* by Dutch priest Henri Nouwen.

"A part of you was left behind very early in your life: that part that never felt completely received. It is full of fears.

Meanwhile, you grew up with many survival skills. But, you want yourself to be whole.

So you have to bring home the part of you that was left behind. That is not easy, because you have become quite the formidable person, and your fearful part does not know if it can safely dwell with you. Your grown-up self has to become very childlike–hospitable, gentle, and caring–so your anxious self can return and feel safe...

As long as your vulnerable self does not feel welcomed by you, it keeps so distant that it cannot show you its true beauty and wisdom. Thus, you survive without really living.

Try to keep your small, fearful self close to you.

This is going to be a struggle, because you have to live for a while with the 'not yet.' Your deepest, truest self is not yet home. It quickly gets scared.

Since your intimate self does not feel safe with you, it continues to look for others, especially those who offer it some real, though temporary, consolation. But when you become more childlike, it will no longer feel the need to dwell elsewhere. It will begin to look to you as home. Be patient.

When you feel lonely, stay with your loneliness. Avoid the temptation to let your fearful self run off. Let it teach you its wisdom; let it tell you that you can live instead of just surviving.

Gradually, you will become whole."

May we not just survive in this world but truly live.

CHAPTER FOUR

LET ME HEAR YOUR BODY TALK

Gut. Bodily. Instinct. Visceral. Intuitive. Anarchy.

Okay, maybe not the last one. But, the rest of these are words that could be used to describe the Eight.

According to the Enneagram, there are 3 types of intelligence: mind, heart, and body (or gut).

Each of these centers inform us about the world around us through our thoughts, feelings, and senses (or intuitions). These centers are *somewhere* in your body telling you *something* whether that's your head, heart, or gut.

For head types, their brains tell them something about the world. They think it in their heads.

For heart types, their hearts feed them information about the world. They feel it in their hearts.

For body types, their guts pick up on information about the world. They sense it in their bodies.

Recent discoveries have shown us that there's neuron activity in the brain, the heart, and the gut.

Isn't that nuts? This is one of the reasons why gut health has become such a huge trend lately.

The Eight, as mentioned above, is in the body (or gut) triad with Enneagram Nines and Enneagram Ones.

In the Enneagram, each type generally has one dominant center, one repressed center, and one center with some access. For Eights, we are feeling repressed. This means that we easily can access our bodies and minds but can struggle to access our hearts.

However, our dominant center is in our gut. From this center, we have a strong intuition about our environment. We trust our gut. It's intuitive, instinctual, and usually subconscious.

We do things "because it just seems right." We act on bodily impulse to stimuli rather than slowing down to think or to feel the emotions of the situation. A lot of the time, our intuition is right—even if it takes days or weeks to see exactly how it was right.

This is why Eights are great in crisis situations. When other types need time to think and feel out the situation, Eights jump into action. Eights are the ones that rise to the occasion when crisis hits.

There is so much to discuss about the Eight and their bodies, but let's start with my favorite aspect: anger.

The Anger That Protects

In the body triad, anger and control is a big deal.

Eights have easy access to anger and often overdo anger, as they generally overdo everything. They will move instinctively to express their anger before they even stop to think about why they are angry in the first place.

Eights also have the most unlimited energy out of all the types on the Enneagram. They can go from an intense workout straight into an emotion filled conversation and then into a board game night without skipping a beat. Their energy is unmatched.

One of the reasons for this energy is the Eight's easy access to anger. Anger is one of the best emotions to channel motivation and energy from. Some psychologists would even argue that anger is an energy not an emotion. Since anger is a secondary, surface emotion, it is typically responding to primary emotions that are deeper underneath the surface.

For Eights, it seems as if their anger, energy, and even sadness is all connected.

I call this the "sadness to anger to energy renewal cycle."

The cycle goes like this:

An Eight gets rejected, betrayed, or hurt in some kind of way. Instead of feeling those sad, soft emotions, the Eight gets angry to protect themselves from feeling those things.

This anger, when stirred and stewed, gets quickly converted into energy.

The Eight will then act out with their new energy, whether by directly fighting the problem or through some form of energy release in their body.

After their energy is expended, they might start to feel those sad, soft emotions again. But, if the Eight is unhealthy, this then kicks in the cycle all over again.

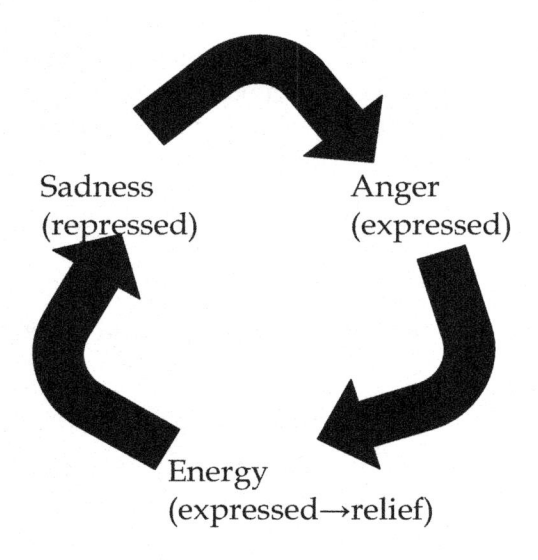

Sadness (repressed) → Anger (expressed) → Energy (expressed→relief) →

The crazy thing about this is that it is all subconscious. Eights are just all of the sudden angry and full of energy but don't realize they're really just sad. Big sad.

Let me explain in a real-life scenario.

Let's imagine that you are an Eight. As life does, it throws shit your way from time to time.

In this case, let's pretend that your partner cheated on you and you just found out about it.

What emotions do you feel? Where do you feel them in your body? Can you feel the anger starting to bubble up? Can you feel the energy coursing from your gut through your heart and into your fists?

That's good. I can too.

For average health Eights, anger is their response to most things. But, just like in the scenario above, anger is often playing the role of a protective emotion.

What would you really be feeling deep down if your partner cheated on you?

You would feel rejected. Hurt. Devastated. Unwanted. Unlovable. Unchosen.

Does that sound like anger to you? No. Those are emotions based in sadness. Emotions based on sorrow.

But, since those emotions are way too scary for Eight types, anger comes in to help take care of it.

Instead of feeling devastating sadness, you feel rage.

Instead of feeling rejection, you feel frustration.

Instead of feeling betrayal, you feel wrath.

Instead of feeling abandonment, you feel fury.

Anger is protecting us. Anger, when left unchecked and unworked through, is numbing us.

Since Anger is an energy too, most Eights often workout when they are sad. Not because they feel sadness, but because their anger has gotten them so jacked up with energy that they need to get it out—we will talk more about using exercise and high intensity workouts to get in touch with softer emotions later.

Overall, it is super important for an Eight to figure out how to get more in touch with those below-the-surface emotions. If the only emotion you feel is anger as an Eight, then you have much work to do.

Since this isn't quite the chapter to work on things yet–that's chapter 8–I will simply leave you with a clip from the *Fresh Prince of Bel-Air* television show that can bring you solidarity in that anger protecting sadness reality.

This clip is one of the most quintessential Eight clips I have ever seen. Just go to YouTube and search "Fresh Prince of Bel-Air - Will's Father Leaves."

I have had many moments like this in my life: where I want to scream and yell and get revenge until I cry.

It's moments like when a young toddler punches and punches his dad in the stomach until they break down into tears from exhaustion. Moments of wanting to run as far away as you can until your body collapses. Moments of wanting to destroy things until you have nothing left.

I watch this *Fresh Prince* clip every once in a while when I want to be reminded of my own stories like this one, or when I just want to cry. I'm literally crying right now as I rewatch it while writing this book.

For real, if you haven't stopped reading this and watched that clip, you NEED to. NOW.

Then, you can keep reading.

Your Body Keeps Score

In his groundbreaking book "The Body Keeps the Score," Bressel van der Kolk talks about how we can store memories and trauma in our bodies.

Due to trauma or stress on the body, our brains can rewire certain areas without you even consciously knowing it.

Although I do not have time to dive into all the details of this, van der Kolk's work has greatly impacted my inner work as an Eight. It helped me see that there was more going on than just what my brain consciously thought.

My body kept the score of my life's experiences.

Our need to be against as an Eight and our natural adversarial nature can turn against ourselves with our bodies. We see our body as something to be conquered, built, or denied. The body has limits, and we cannot deal with limits, so we push our bodies beyond these limits. When we push past these limits, we often open ourselves up to trauma and immense stress.

This came out for me so clearly on October 11, 2021.

I got the call at 8:45pm.

The call that every single person dreads. The call that your body always knew was a possibility, but your mind and heart never wanted to believe it.

My good friend—we'll call him John—had sent a suicide letter to his therapist with intention of taking his own life with a weapon.

I can remember rushing over to his apartment that was about 20 minutes from mine. Adrenaline and dread pulsating through my body.

I knew what I was heading to.

My brain hoped he would still be alive. My heart wished he would still be breathing. My body knew what was coming.

For some odd reason, the cops weren't at his apartment and weren't coming anytime soon. I could see my other friends who had shown up standing around and trying to figure out what to do.

Instinctively, I knew we were faced with a decision: do we go in ourselves to check on him or do we wait for the cops to come?

As an Eight, I knew exactly what my answer was.

My body also knew what the answer was, and it hated it. If there's a 1% chance our friend was alive, we had to check on him.

In other words, we were going in. I was going in. I was going to face death.

My body was going to face death.

I got to his apartment door that I had been to many times before. But, this time was different. I didn't know what was on the other side. For reasons I won't share here, I knew there was a chance that my own life might end that night as well.

I was standing at the door. I knew death was waiting for me on the other side. My death, his death, depravity itself.

My body was panicking and screaming within me, "Don't do this. Don't go in. Wait for the cops. Find another way. Anything but this."

I told my body to shut up.

We must do this. We must do the hard things that we don't want to do. We have to be the ones to find out. We have to be the ones to face this. We are the only ones that can do this.

With that, my brain and my body severed in their connection. My body turned off. My brain went in.

And it was just as we thought: death was in the room.

John was gone.

Amidst the next month of funeral planning and sharing the news with his family and friends, my body never came back on.

I was a floating brain. I was a beating heart. I was not an embodied being.

It wasn't until about a month after John's death that my body rebooted and reconnected to the rest of me. In that reconnection, came the terror of that night.

It was like my body finally came back to life and just started screaming. My body was still in that room with death.

I started having panic attacks every few days where my body would replay the sensations of that night. I had debilitating and disorienting anxiety even when my brain was blank. My right hand, the hand that opened the door, developed a tremor. I would wake up in the middle of the night in a dead sweat with fear pulsating through my body. Certain sights, sounds, and smells brought on panic.

My body was revolting against me.

I was eventually diagnosed with post-traumatic stress disorder.

This disorder—my disorder—was a disorder of the body. My body kept the score of that night and replayed it on repeat for months. My body was still in that room, even when my brain tried to tell it we weren't.

My body remembered that night. My body carried the stress. My body held the trauma.

There are obviously many things that were crazy about this season. But for the sake of this chapter, I'll focus on my body.

As Eights, we carry things in our bodies. We are instinctual. We feel things deep in our bowels and just know them to be right. We might not be able to explain why this is, but we feel in our bones what is right and what is wrong.

Since Eights also feel the need to push themselves, they will become comfortable putting themselves in harm's way. It becomes a part of the identity of the Eight to conquer and dominate their bodies–this is especially true of repressed Self-Preservation Eights.

Eight's bodies know that they can't handle it, but the Eight's will and mind tell them to push through it.

This is where trauma happens.

Often, Eights aren't aware of the trauma they carry in their bodies. Eights don't take harm or trauma seriously unless it's a huge deal. So, Eights are typically blind to their own trauma.

However, trauma is there. It's especially there in their bodies.

For Eights, it's important for us to learn what we're carrying in our bodies.

Are we carrying past trauma? Were we harmed by someone else, or did we harm ourselves? Are we currently harming our bodies by pushing them past their limits? Have we sought to conquer our bodies rather than cherish them?

One of the biggest ways Eights push their bodies past their limits is through the Eight's need for intensity.

Intensity in Everything

If you've ever known an Eight, one of the few things you've probably noticed about them is their intensity.

Their intense stare. Their intense workout regimen. Their intense conversations. Their intense life.

Everything is intense.

In relation to intensity, Eights might also be the loudest of all the personality types. Loud voices. Loud clothing choices. Loud conversations. Loud lives.

Although intensity in other areas should be dissected–specifically the Eight's lust and need for excess–we will focus mostly on our bodily intensity in this chapter. Namely, the Eight's physical exertion through activities and work.

The Eight body needs intensity. Whether that's working out till you collapse, having a sexathon, reading a book until their eyes burn, or going on a 20-mile hike just for kicks, the Eight craves intensity.

This can lead to exhaustion or even injury. I've hurt myself countless times working out by grinding my body into the ground and ignoring the normal warning signs of pain.

One of my favorite phrases is "whatever kills me makes me stronger." My friends love working out with me.

I know many other Eights that also get injured while working out. On top of this, most Eights will refuse to see a doctor.

I honestly can't tell you the last time I went to a doctor for a check-up. It has been close to 10 years. Unless a bone is literally broken or I've cut off my finger, I refuse to get help from a doctor.

As I'm writing this, I severely pulled a muscle in my back to the point that I can hardly walk. It's been like this for three days.

Am I going to see a doctor? Absolutely not.

Will I be back in the gym in a day? Probably.

I can figure it out myself. I'll take care of myself. I don't need a doctor.

It might be safe to say that we're at war with our bodies. We push them to their limits and often past their limits.

We tell our bodies that they have another gear, they have more in the tank, and that they can go farther than they think. We have this internal voice shouting at us to do one more rep, one more mile, or one more sprint.

My Nanu is a perfect example of an Eight who believes they can switch gears and grind themselves to accomplish whatever they want. Nanu honestly believes that if he puts his mind and body to something, he can do it.

When he was 60 years old, Nanu decided to quit smoking and drinking and start running marathons. No bullshit. He really did that.

He went from a chain-smoker and someone who hardly worked out to literally running marathons with 20-year-olds. He ended up running 5 marathons after the age of 60 in only a 2-year span. Once his body couldn't run full marathons anymore, he ran an additional 10 half marathons.

He's now working at a golf course doing manual labor at 84 years old. The dude works 60 hours a week out in the Arizona heat. He's absolutely bonkers.

But hey, that's just what it means to be an Eight.

Like my Grandpa Nanu, this bodily intensity doesn't just end with physically working out. The Eight's intensity also comes out in other places.

In the workplace, the Eight workload might be larger than any other number. Most are amazed at how much an Eight accomplishes. Quite frankly, Eights get shit done.

Eights are the classic type to grind through their career until their body, their mind, or their relationships give out. It is normally only when this happens that an Eight might reevaluate their work pace.

No matter what industry an Eight is in, no matter what kind of thing they are doing, there is a good chance they are the most intense person on the team.

Sometimes, this intensity is a beautiful thing. It can inspire those around them.

But other times, it is a destructive force to themselves and others. It is necessary for an Eight to learn how to love their body and channel their intensity well.

Through intensity in the workplace and intensity in other areas, Eights can lose touch with other aspects of being.

They lose touch with their hearts. They lose touch with their loved ones. They lose touch with themselves. They just grind away.

As you can imagine, this does great damage to their personal lives.

An Eight might be the best employee at their company, but the worst father. They might be the strongest person in the gym, but their hearts are giving out due to stress. They might be the king of networking at their job but go home to detached relationships in their friends and family.

This is why it is so vital for Eights to find outlets for their intensity. Intensity can keep them from vulnerability and tenderness just like their anger can–more on that later.

There is one more important thing worth mentioning about intensity.

For a lot of Eights, intensity has actually been a tough reality. Especially for female Eights and Eight wing Nines, they have often felt like they were "too much." They felt like they had to rein their intensity in for others. Their intensity wasn't good.

If anything, intensity was bad. Very bad.

For these Eights, it will be important to discover that intensity is a neutral force.

It is neither good nor bad. It can be a source of a great good in the lives of those around you. Or, it can be a damaging and destructive force.

Being an intense person isn't bad.

It is simply what we do with intensity that determines what kind of force we become.

Befriend Your Body to Befriend Your Heart

I know.

Really CV? Befriend your heart? Have you become a fucking softie on us?

From my experience, the harder we are as Eights, the harder those around us treat us. I don't know about you, but I don't like it when everyone is on their guard around me and treats me like I'm some heartless prick.

We need to befriend our hearts. We need to learn how to discover our emotions. We need to learn how to bring that tender self forward without fully protecting it.

One way we can do this is by befriending our body.

This might look like learning how to use our bodies well and not neglecting them. It could look like being tender to our injuries and not pushing ourselves past our limits. Most importantly, it might look like finding outlets for our body's intensity.

One of the biggest needs we have is to get our intensity out so we're not just yelling at everyone around us at all times. Since Eights often connect through intensity, they can ramp up their intensity and passion when they feel disconnected.

In my life, I can normally gauge how secure I feel in my relationships by how much intensity I force into my life and my friends' lives.

If you ask my friends, this tendency can be destructive for our friendships because people don't like being cornered and challenged for no damn reason.

How would you feel as an Eight if someone did that to you? Yeah, not ideal. We'd probably punch them in the throat.

Since Eights are body types, their emotions are normally hiding behind their bodies. Therefore, it is essential for Eights to find places to discharge their built-up intensity so that their heart can come out.

Therefore, finding your intensity outlets is key.

Your intensity outlet could be joining a kickboxing gym. It could be running marathons. It could be doing justice work on the weekends. It could be writing a book on the Eight. Just something. Something intense. Something that drains it all out of your body.

For me, I usually will try and workout as hard as I can (without injuring myself) until my emotions start flowing.

My routine is to play epic instrumental battle music and do sprints until I start crying or feel emotions other than anger. For real, I do this. Ask any of the people who work out near me at my local Planet Fitness.

If you are an Eight reading this, it is important to find out what your intensity outlets are and use them. Trust me, your friends and loved ones will appreciate the Eight that comes back from those outlets. They will appreciate that you are a little gentler, a little more tender, and a little less antagonistic.

It is also vitally important for us to learn our bodies' limits.

You know all that stuff I said earlier about how we grind ourselves into the ground? Yeah, that's not a good thing.

Sure, getting our intensity out is one thing. But, there are many times when our bodies are shouting at us that they can't do it anymore. That they don't want to do another rep. That they're tired, exhausted, and on the brink of unraveling.

In my story above with my friend's suicide, I had pushed my body past its' limits in that season. Because of that, it came crashing down.

It's okay some days to take a walk instead of a run. It's okay to only workout for twenty minutes rather than two hours. It's okay to finish that project the next day. It's okay to not expend yourself to help that needy person or confront that arrogant person. It's okay to be kind to yourself and your body.

We need to learn how to regain our hearts. We need to learn how to let our hearts show rather than just our bodies and our will. We need to be a human—one that exists in body, mind, AND heart.

This is extremely important because most Eights have a deep sense of sorrow within them. I've heard so many Eights recount "I am scared that if I start crying, I will never stop."

For Eights, we need to find healing for these places of sorrow. We need to find healing for our "Switch" moments. It's often impossible to find this healing while our bodies are raging with anger and energy. We have to first work through our body in order to allow the sadness to rise to the surface.

I don't know what it is for you. I am not sure how you can best love your body. I don't know what your intensity outlets will be. I don't know the exact path for you to allow your heart to come out.

But, find them. Discover your limits. Be gentle to yourself. Love your body well.

Your friends and loved ones will thank you for it.

There's so much stored in our bodies.

Trauma. Memories. Emotions. Energy. Pizza (at least for me).

For most of us, we are completely unaware that these things are even there.

It's super important for Eights to become aware of their bodies.

If an Eight is angry and full of energy all the time, then they need to slow down, take some deep breaths, and dive underneath their anger.

Just trust me on this one.

CHAPTER FIVE

FAITH AND EIGHT

The Enneagram has become increasingly popular in religious circles in recent years.

Some argue that it is a great tool for self-exploration to become more like the Divine. Others have argued that it is rooted in the occult and should be avoided at all costs.

I'm not here to make a claim either way. You have your own beliefs and ideas about things. Good for you.

However, if you honestly believed the Enneagram is irredeemable because of its origins, then you wouldn't be here reading this book, would you?

If you are afraid of the Enneagram because of its possible occult origins, then are you also afraid of Christmas because of its pagan origins? You do know that Christians hijacked the winter solstice of drunkenness and sex and turned it into a birthday party for Jesus, right? Can we not do the same thing with the Enneagram?

So, I'll just assume you're okay with the Enneagram and address the rest of you all.

Some of you Eights might be religious zealots or religious leaders. Some of you might hate religion entirely and think it's full of insecure men in robes. Some of you might be passionately indifferent to it.

As Eights, we take our beliefs and convictions seriously. I fully understand that some of you might hate the fact that there is a faith chapter at all in this book. For others, this book wouldn't be complete without it.

For those who are religious, this section will help you take your understanding of yourself to another level. For those who aren't, I still believe there are gems in here even if you don't buy the whole God thing.

For those who aren't religious, you can also just skip this chapter.

Your call. I know I can't convince you regardless.

Now that we've gotten rid of the pagans, let's talk about faith and Eights.

To be perfectly honest, I am a follower of Jesus–in other words, I am a Christian.

I'm not one of those normal Christians though. You won't find me in a pew or in a chapel. You won't see me preaching outside an abortion clinic or demanding tithing from poor people to fund my upper-middle class dreams. And I sure as hell don't partake in the Christianity of big buildings and big budgets that neglect the poor and needy around us.

It's okay, I know you don't either right? I'm sure your church and your version of Christianity is the good one, just like mine.

I do Christianity and Church in a house, around a meal, with those who live in my neighborhood. I try (often unsuccessfully) to do Jesus stuff like Jesus did: healing, feeding, helping, sacrificing, and hanging out with outsiders.

I'm still trying to figure out what this whole thing means. I'm still wondering what's the best way to love my neighbor without participating in the greed and exploitation of my age. In many ways, I'm still struggling to have my actions match my values.

So, don't put me in a box of what a Christian means or doesn't mean to you. Fuck your box.

All that to say, this section is going to be coming from a Christian perspective. Most of the stories will be centered around the life and teachings of Jesus of Nazareth. However, I do believe other non-Christian faiths can resonate with some of the themes we will be discussing.

Let's dive into some of my favorite faith stories that relate to being an Eight.

Jesus' "Eight" Moment

Growing up, there was always one story in the Bible that spoke to me.

It spoke to this visceral part of me. It spoke directly to my body and my pent-up rage.

The story goes like this, *"When it was almost time for the Jewish Passover, Jesus went up to Jerusalem. In the temple courts he found people selling cattle, sheep and doves, and others sitting at tables exchanging money. So he made a whip out of cords, and drove all from the temple courts, both sheep and cattle; he scattered the coins of the money changers and overturned their tables. To those who sold doves he said, 'Get these out of here! Stop turning my Father's house into a market!'"* (John 2:13-16).

I fucking love this story.

Jesus was such a badass. Enough of that love your enemies shit, this is the kind of stuff I like to see!

The more I dove into this story when I was in Bible college, the more I fell in love with it. I always pictured Jesus walking up and seeing this scene unfolding. After looking it over, he immediately runs in with this whip that he pulled out of his tunic and just starts smacking the shit out of everyone.

The actual story is even better.

Most people skim over this part, but if you go back to the story you will see it. Jesus didn't just bring a whip out of his robes that he already had. He *made a whip*. This dude literally *made* it.

Now, I know we're living in the age where you can just order a whip on Amazon–I just searched "whips" as I was writing this and boy, there are lots of different kinds of whips for different uses (mostly sexual) on Amazon.

However, Jesus didn't have Amazon. So, he made the whip himself.

Can you picture that?

Jesus, seeing the injustice happening in the temple courts, sits down and slowly makes a whip out of different cords.

I can just imagine him sitting there, seething as he weaves these cords together. Thinking of which people he's going to charge at first. Thinking of the snappy one liner he might say as he clears them out. Picturing the looks on their faces when he runs in there and starts going apeshit.

I can totally relate to this Jesus. This Jesus speaks to us Eights.

He sees injustice happening and he acts.

The age-old injustice of the religious elite making a profit off the poor and vulnerable in society. In the place where they should be serving the poor, they are stealing from them.

This whole scene pisses him off. He drives the thieves out. He throws their precious coins on the ground. He flips over their greedy tables. He calls them "a den of robbers."

This is a God I can believe in. Where his anger is kindled towards injustice. Where he tears down the corrupt. Where he fights the "high and mighty" and raises up the "low and powerless."

There is a place for our anger, Eights. There is something beautiful about it. It is needed.

We clearly see the injustice happening all around us that everyone else has become numb to.

We burn with zeal for things to be made right. We feel it in our bones. We feel it in our gut. We must act. We must make things just.

Even if we have to do it alone, we will fight for what's right.

Don't let others dampen your view of God that he never gets angry. Don't let corrupt religious leaders who are profiting off their people convince you that your anger towards them is unfounded and sinful. Don't let passive people tell you that you need to always be peaceful and gentle.

There are times when anger is necessary. There are times when loud voices and bodily demonstrations are necessary. There are times when we need to speak up, stand out, and call down people and systems.

This kind of anger actually draws people to us. When we cast down oppressive structures, we free those oppressed by them. Even in this story of Jesus, the blind and lame come to home after he clears out the temple. His righteous anger created a space for those most vulnerable. This is the kind of anger Eights strive to have.

Our anger is beautiful. Our anger is godly. Our anger is like Jesus.

Well, sometimes it is. As I'm sure you know, we're not justified every time we get angry.
We will discuss another story about that kind of anger. For this one, just know that your anger can be a source of action for justice.

Your anger can be righteous.

Swords and Revenge

One of my most hated passages in the Bible comes in Matthew 5:38-39.

Jesus says, *"You have heard that it was said, 'Eye for eye, and tooth for tooth.' But I tell you, do not resist an evil person. If anyone slaps you on the right cheek, turn to them the other cheek also."*

What the hell? I get that Jesus was a good guy and all, but what the fuck is this shit? Wasn't this the dude with the whip?

This advice isn't fair. It isn't just. It isn't right.

I can remember being caught in a situation like this before. *When I was about 11 years old, my friend Alex and I were hanging out at my house.*

It was a normal Saturday where we were playing a lot of Halo 3 and munching on junk food.

Around midday, we ran out of snacks. So, we went to my kitchen pantry to look for something to keep shoving down our throats as we killed aliens.

In my pantry, there was a box of my favorite snack: Goldfish crackers. I loved Goldfish. I would kill for Goldfish.

As I reached for the Goldfish, I was feeling a little cocky about how our last game went. So, I remarked over my shoulder "I hear that the Goldfish can only be eaten by winners in this house."

I know, I was such a remarkable shit talker in my youth.

After I said this, Alex slapped me straight across the back of my head. Without even thinking about it, I turned and slapped him straight across the face.

With this, the battle had begun. Alex then slapped me again and ran. I chased after him until I cornered him and slapped him as hard as I could across the face again. This slap battle continued throughout the house like a game of tag with each person running away after they got their last slap in. We both wanted to have the last word, the last slap.

Eventually, we both tired out from running and from the pain in our jaws. Needless to say, this was the first fight I had ever been in–if you could even call it that.

Even though this is a rather childish story, it can stand as a metaphor for a lot of our adult encounters.

Someone writes something snarky on social media, you respond with something even sassier. Someone cuts you off in traffic, you flip them off, cuss them out, and contemplate the financial cost of ramming into them. A coworker acts entitled and privileged, so you talk shit behind their back and think of ways to sabotage them. A family member is being stubborn and unreasonable, so you dig in your heels as well. Someone calls you a shithead, so you call them a fuckface.

Revenge is all around us. "Getting even" is in the water we drink. Fighting fire with fire is our strategy for life.

Wasn't I justified in hitting Alex back? What's wrong with giving someone a taste of their own medicine? Isn't that what's right?

I like the saying of "an eye for an eye." That makes much more sense to me.

So, why did Jesus tell us to not get even? Why would he make that a point of emphasis in one of his most famous teachings?

There's a story later in the life of Jesus that fleshes out this point more clearly.

It's best to tell this story from the point of view of Peter, one of Jesus' disciples. I'll use first person pronouns to flesh out the story.

I can remember this story like it was yesterday, especially considering what happened after it.

There we were. Jesus, James, John, and I praying in this garden– well, Jesus was praying at least. The rest of us were resting our eyes for a bit.

Suddenly, I awoke to the sound of feet coming towards us. And it sounded like a LOT of them.

I could slowly start to see torches and a group of soldiers marching right toward us. I was worried this would happen one day. I had been telling Jesus we should be more careful. I knew they were out to get us.

As they got closer, I realized I saw a familiar face among them: Judas.

Judas? Our friend and fellow disciple? I don't understand.

We were just with him some hours ago. Why does it look like he's leading this group of soldiers right to us?

Jesus, being the person that he is, asked them, "Who are you looking for?" And I'm sitting here like, "Isn't it obvious, Jesus?"

They responded and said they were looking for "Jesus of Nazareth." Under my breath, I muttered, "No shit."

It was at this moment that I truly realized what was happening. These dudes were here to arrest Jesus. They were going to take him.

To our demise, it looked like there was nothing we could do about it. We were cornered.
As they started to come towards us, I remembered the sword I always kept at my side. Far be it from us to go down without a fight!

With this, I took my sword out and swung it at the first soldier's head. Since I am merely a fisherman turned disciple, I managed to only slice off the soldier's ear.

But, second times the charm right? With that, I raised up my sword to strike again. Just as I was about to cut this dude's head off, Jesus yelled at me, "All who draw the sword will die by the sword."

What? Doesn't Jesus know what's happening? Doesn't he know that when you are cornered like this you have to fight back?

They brought swords. Why can't we use ours? These people have been oppressing us for years with swords, and now he's scolding me because I'm giving them a taste of their own medicine.

To top it all off, Jesus walks over and literally heals this guy's severed ear right in front of me.

As for the rest of the story, I am not a huge fan of talking about what's next. Maybe another time.

I like to tell this story from Peter's perspective because he's a stand-in for an Enneagram Eight in this scenario—even though he was probably a Seven Wing Eight.

Peter, like an Eight, noticed the imbalance of power. He realized that they were backed against a wall. He channeled his fear into action. He attacked instead of fleeing.

This is what Eight's do when they are cornered: they charge at you with their swords.

Jesus' actions are different than an Eights. They tell us a different story about what to do when we are attacked.

We love. We forgive. We sacrifice ourselves. We seek to bless. We heal the wounds we have caused.

Jesus understood something that us Eights often don't understand: that violence begets violence.

Jesus knew that evil follows itself in a vicious cycle. That when we feel attacked and want to attack back, we only perpetuate the cycle of evil rather than fix it. When we respond to evil with evil, we ourselves become a part of the problem.

Martin Luther King Jr., an Enneagram Eight, remarked, "Darkness cannot drive out darkness; only light can do that. Hate cannot drive out hate; only love can do that."

We want to fix injustice, right? We want to rid this world of violence and evil, correct? We want to see the end of oppression, don't we?

These desires are good ones, but we must be careful with what tools we use to fight evil.

If we use a sword, then we will be countered with swords. If we use authoritarianism, then we will be ruled over eventually. We will become a victim to the very thing we think we need to use to set us free.

This is the path that Jesus calls us Eights to.

To not act on impulse and respond in the way our vengeful heart craves. To not seek revenge at every turn. To not slap your friend back in the face no matter how much he may deserve it.

Rather, our call is to respond to attacks on us with love. To respond to swords with sacrifice. To respond to hate with forgiveness.

The way towards justice is to love our enemies. To bless those who curse us. To lay down our swords and heal those who are harmed.

This is the healthy path of the Eight.

Unrighteous Anger

Remember earlier how I said we would talk about our anger when it isn't justified?

Here we are.

Let me share a parable from 2,000 years ago.

"The kingdom of heaven is like a man who sowed good seed in his field. But while everyone was sleeping, his enemy came and sowed weeds among the wheat, and went away. When the wheat sprouted and formed heads, then the weeds also appeared. The owner's servants came to him and said, 'Sir, didn't you sow good seed in your field? Where then did the weeds come from?'

'An enemy did this,' he replied.

The servants asked him, 'Do you want us to go and pull them up?'

'No,' he answered, 'because while you are pulling the weeds, you may uproot the wheat with them. Let both grow together until the harvest. At that time I will tell the harvesters: First collect the weeds and tie them in bundles to be burned; then gather the wheat and bring it into my barn.'" (Matthew 13:24-30).

Sometimes in our anger against the evils of the world, we mistakenly attack goodness. We burn the whole farm down rather than just the weeds. We rip out good things by taking out the bad things.

If there were one parable about how our pursuit for justice goes astray, it is this.

I cannot tell you how many times I have hurt those around me by trying to protect them. I cannot tell you how many times I have torn down good ideas while I rampaged against the bad ones. I cannot tell you how many times I have been indiscriminate in my pursuit of justice.

There will be moments when we truly need to rip out the weeds. When these moments come, everyone will look to Eights to do this very thing.

In the meantime, we must learn to let both good and bad grow together. We must be careful to not stomp on goodness while we strike down evil. We must be wise in not destroying healthy things while we take down unhealthy ones.

Pursuing justice is a delicate and precise endeavor.

We are not called to be like the Liam Neeson character in Taken where you just indiscriminately murder every guy in your way. We cannot be John Wick and destroy every person in our path. I know people love them, but we really can't be any of those other white-guy-revenge movies either.

To truly pursue righteous anger and justice, we must be immensely careful when we go gather up the weeds. If we aren't, there will be a trail of bodies behind us of good and innocent people.

Our anger can be good. Our anger can propel us towards justice. Our anger can be a catalyzer for equality.

Our anger can also blind us. Our anger can cause us to attack everyone rather than just the guilty parties. Our anger can cause great harm to good people.

May we be Eights that control our anger to use it for justice and not destruction.

The Ultimate Betrayal

Enough about anger.

I'm sure we all get it now. Bad anger is bad and good anger is good. Pretty remarkable stuff here. So, I'm sure many of you are like, "Tell us something we don't know, Bitch."

Challenge accepted.

Let's talk about betrayal. The Eight's favorite.

Jesus knew a thing or two about betrayal. No, he never had his heart broken by a girl who ended up cheating on him with a local goat herder (that we know of). Rather, his story climaxes with one of the most devastating portrayals of betrayal I have ever seen in fiction or nonfiction.

For those who may not be familiar with the story, Jesus spent most of his life being a stone smith (not a carpenter, look it up idiots). Towards the end of his life, he embarked on a mission of teaching those around him about God and life itself, while healing those who needed healing.

He did this for three years with a group of twelve disciples and many others accompanying him. Towards the end of his life, he had pissed off a good amount of people, especially the religious elite. So, they did what all religious elites have done for centuries and eliminated him.

Right before his crucifixion, he had some shit go down with his closest followers. That shit is what we want to talk about in this section.

In the moments leading up to Jesus' death, he had his closest friends betray him, deny him, and abandon him. In the moment of his greatest need for friends and allies, they all let him down. The best effort he got out of his closest friends was Peter cutting off a soldier's ear, but we already talked about that.

If this had happened to me, I don't know what I would have done. I can't imagine losing all my closest friends like this. I can't imagine what it would feel like to have them all turn their backs on me. I've had one girlfriend cheat on me, and it felt like I could never trust anyone ever again. I just simply can't imagine.

However, this story is most remarkable to me because of what happens right before this betrayal. Many of you know this moment as "The Last Supper."

The night before Jesus' death, he had a big meal with his closest friends.

At this point in his life, Jesus knew that he was going to be betrayed, abandoned, and killed because of his friends. Yet, he still came to this dinner.

As an Eight, could you imagine that?

You know that there's people in this room who are liars. People who are going to backstab you. Who are going to deny they even know you. Who are going to abandon you when they could have saved you. Who are going to leave you when you need them the most.

What would you do? How would you act? What would you say?

I know what I would do.

I would have been seething about it all day and ready to pop off at dinner. I'd have my moves planned, my words crafted, and my responses prepared. I would be ready to throw down, whether physically or verbally.

Yet, Jesus didn't do that. He chose to wash their feet instead.

What? Why? And why feet? Isn't that weird, Jesus? Does he have some kind of foot fetish or something?

Just to remind everyone, Jesus was a Middle Eastern man from 2,000 years ago. He wasn't a millennial sipping on a $6 latte at his local Starbucks, living in some gentrified metropolitan city. His culture was based in hospitality. It was traditional to wash your guests' feet when they entered the house, especially before dinner time when their feet would be getting near the food.

It's important here that we pause and talk about those feet. Don't get too excited, Podofilias. These won't be sexy feet.

In Jesus' day, they wore sandals and didn't have socks. On top of that, they didn't have plumbing either.

Can you guess where the shit went? Out on the streets.

So, when they walked around in sandals, what do you think they were walking around in?

Yeah, you're getting it now. These feet were nasty as hell.

On Jesus' last night, the night before his death, the night of his greatest betrayal, the night of his friend's denying him and abandoning him, he put a towel around his waist, grabbed a water bowl, and washed their feet.

He took the dirt and shit from their feet and cleaned it off. In doing this, he literally took their dirt onto himself.

On Jesus' night of betrayal, he served his betrayers.

He encouraged his deserters. He comforted his liars. He calmed the fears and worries of those who would deny they knew him. He loved those who hated him.

To top it all off, when Jesus resurrects and visits his disciples, he embraces them. He forgives them. He reinstates Peter in John 21. He calms Thomas' doubts in John 20.

When he should be giving them the middle finger and telling them, "I told you so," Jesus is instead compassionate, forgiving, and healing to them.

What would it take for an Eight to respond to betrayal like this in this situation?

We'll discuss more of that in chapter 8.

For now, your homework from this section is to read the Gospel of Luke and notice how often forgiveness is mentioned.

I know forgiveness is hard. I know people are truly undeserving of our forgiveness. But, forgiving others is the path to freedom from our vengeful cycles.

Be the Last

Finally, the Divine calls the Eight to serve.

As you will see later, the Eight takes on Enneagram Two qualities when we are secure.

For those who don't know, Twos are the helpers of the enneagram. At their best, they are selfless, altruistic, and love others unconditionally.

For Eights, we need to learn how to discover what it means to serve. To put others' needs and wants ahead of our own. To truly let others be a priority over us, even when we disagree with them deeply.

In this instance, Jesus of Nazareth has more wisdom for us.

Matthew 20:25 says, *"Jesus called them together and said, 'You know that the rulers of the Gentiles lord it over them, and their high officials exercise authority over them. Not so with you. Instead, whoever wants to become great among you must be your servant, and whoever wants to be first must be your servant—just as the Son of Man did not come to be served, but to serve, and to give his life as a ransom for many.'"*

What would it look like for an Eight to take this passage to heart? What would it look like to be the least? What would it look like to serve and not be served?

In Jesus' life and ministry, much of his teaching was centered around this upside-down thinking.

To be the greatest, you become the least. The last end up first, the first end up last. The best way to be powerful is to give it all up. The way to life is through choosing death.

Just so much paradoxical, upside-down stuff.

However, I am not going to sit here and rant about how Eights shouldn't lead. Some of our most misunderstood times are when it feels like people are accusing us of being authoritarians when we are genuinely trying to help them or an organization.

I am with you, Eights. I get it.

Most of the time, our intentions are good. We try to lead to keep others safe. We take control to make sure everyone's needs are met. Even when people misunderstand our intentions and actions, I know we truly mean well.

It still begs the question, what would it look like to give up control? What would it take to trust others' leadership? What would it look like to be a servant and not a leader?

For me, it is so damn hard to trust someone else to lead and do a good job. It is so hard to leave the controls of the project to someone else when I know I can do it better or more efficiently. It is hard to allow others to take the lead when they lead so terribly.

Even if it is true that others will lead poorly—which it usually is—there is still some goodness and benefits in letting others lead.

As we talked about earlier, Eights can find rest when someone else is in charge. I would also argue that Eights can find intimacy and connection when they are not leading.

When Eights are in charge, they often lose friendship. They lose connection with others. They lose genuine relationships. Most Eight relationships are with superiors and inferiors. Eventually, Eights end up with no peers.

When an Eight gives up control, forsakes having to lead, and seeks to serve those around them as a peer, they might find the genuine companionship that they have desperately been looking for.

My greatest times of connectedness have been through my times of being least in control and in charge. There's a profound sense of belonging when you become a part of the team rather than the one driving it.

In summary, it's absolutely terrifying to let others lead.

It might even be bad for the economic health of the organization to let others take charge. Yet, it is so incredibly healthy for you as an individual to just be a member on the team rather than a leader in front.

So, learn to serve. Lead from behind. Let others be in charge, even if they're not as competent.

Hell, even switch careers to a job that's more supportive than directive.

I'm not saying you have to be a janitor for the rest of your life but being a janitor doesn't actually sound that bad if I'm in connected, loving, and trustworthy relationships.

Jump into the upside-down nature of leadership. It might change your life.

I believe that there is so much to learn from the spiritual component of our lives.

For Eights, knowing that there might be a Divine being(s) out there can bring us peace. Knowing that there are greater forces at work leading the universe, we can rest in our tiny portion of it. When we realize how vast and expansive the world is, we can worry a little less about who's in charge of our little piece of it.

Some of our Eight qualities are divine. Some of our Eight qualities are human. Some of our Eight qualities are good. Some of our Eight qualities are evil.

In all of this, it is important to remember that we are loved.

CHAPTER SIX

HOW TO NOT BE A DICK TO THE OTHER EIGHT NUMBERS

When I first sat down to write this book, I reached out to many of my Eight friends to see what they would want in an Eight book.

This chapter was the most requested by far.

This either means my friends are trying hard to love others and want to learn more, or they are assholes to those around them and want me to validate them.

Let's just assume it's the former.

Before we get into the specific dynamics with each type, it is important to note that these are generalities–as is this whole book.

If you are a different enneagram type reading this book, don't take it personally if my descriptions don't fit you perfectly. This is a book about the Eight. It's missing the nuances of your specific type.

Helen Palmer's book *The Enneagram in Love and Work* is a phenomenal resource if you would like to dive deeper into the whole of the Enneagram and how they relate to one another. This chapter will be focusing exclusively on the Eight's dynamics with other numbers.

Before we get into the specifics of each type, there are some general realities about the Eight's relationships that are important to discuss here. Each type will share these dynamics with the Eight.

First, Eights see strengths in others that others might not see in themselves. This is why many love being around Eights. Their confidence is infectious. Eights can see your strengths and weaknesses clearly. They can help you work on both of them.

Second, Eights tend to intimidate those around them and hurt others with their blunt language. This one will come up a lot in the descriptions below, especially in the more sensitive numbers. Spoiler: everyone is more sensitive than the Eight. It is important for Eights to learn how to put certain things in a gift box when they talk to people.

Finally, this last generality might be the most important point. When you are engaging with other personality types as an Eight, you need to learn to listen.

Eights often are 10 steps ahead of others in their thought processes. It's been said that if you think things at 1x speed and you feel things at 10x speed, then you instinctively respond to things at 100x speed. So, since Eights are instinct types, they need to learn to slow down for others– themselves!

You can see this reality in my story I shared in chapter 4 when I talked about the night John died.

When I showed up on the scene, I could see my friends who are head and heart types deliberating. The head types wanted to think it through, and the heart types were trying to figure out what they felt. Not for me, I knew what needed to be done. I couldn't articulate it to you then, but I just had this gut feeling of what the right path was.

Because of this speed of processing, it is important for Eights to slow down and truly listen to others. Eights need to learn to simply let people be where they are, even if the Eight is convinced they know where they are headed or foresee the potential pitfalls of their journey.

With all of those in mind, let's dive into the specifics of each type and their relational dynamics with the Eight.

Ones

The Enneagram One is called "the Reformer," "the Perfectionist," or "the Idealist."

Ones are conscientious and ethical. They see the world through a black/white or right/wrong lens. They are teachers, crusaders, and advocates for change.

Ones are always striving to improve things, but afraid of making a mistake. They are usually well-organized and orderly. Maintaining high standards for themselves and others, they can slip into being critical and perfectionistic. They have problems with resentment and impatience.

At their best, Ones are wise, discerning, realistic, joyful, and noble. They can be morally heroic.

At their worst, Ones are critical, angry, resentful, and hypocritical.

What We Love About Ones

Eights admire the power of Ones.

Eights respect the way Ones pursue their convictions and ideals, especially when they agree with them.

Eights, when healthy, love that the Ones value the means just as much as the ends.

What We Hate About Ones

Eights generally view Ones as self-righteous hypocrites.

Eights are furious at the Ones' moral uprightness and idealism. Eights, whether they realize it or not, feel judged by the One's morality even when the One doesn't impose it on them.

Eights can struggle with the headstrongness of Ones. Ones do not usually budge on their ideals which can cause problems for relationships with Eights.

How We Can Relate to Ones

Enneagram expert Helen Palmer describes these two as the Enneagram opposites.

The One and Eight can be the other's worst nightmare. They can both be the bossiest types.

Since they are both anger types, they have tendencies of black-or-white thinking but come to those conclusions through vastly different logic. The One's rigidity can bring out the Eight's desire to "be bad," which in turn can cause the One to double down on their values.

Despite this, Eights can still dominate Ones. Eights need to learn to give space to the Ones to hear them out and not interrupt the One before they can fully respond to them.

Since it's impossible to stop the One once they get going towards their ideals, Eights need to hear the heart of the One. An Eight has to learn to see the heart behind the One's pursuits so they can be more gracious and compassionate to them.

When it comes to the One's idealism, it is important that the Eight learns to adopt some of the ideals that the One holds tightly. If they can't see the good in the One, then it will spell trouble for their whole relationship.

Due to the Eight's naturally antagonistic nature, this next point is especially important. When an Eight criticizes a deeply held value of the One, it can feel like a critique of the One themself. Therefore, it's super important that Eights figure out what ideals their One holds tightly and learn to respect them.

Eights also need to watch the words they use and how they use them. For Ones, tact in communication is super important. They take the time to think through their words and mean exactly what they say. However, as you've learned in this book, Eights can frequently use words flippantly.

This combination can cause flames in their relationship. Since Ones care deeply about the delivery of communication as well as the content itself, Eights can come across brash and crude. Because of this, Eights need to be more mindful with their language in what they say and how they say it. Eights may even need to add softer language and not be as direct in order to communicate effectively with a One.

If you are a One reading this, the Eight wants you to be kinder to them.

I know that sounds bizarre considering how rough you might see Eights as, but it's true. They don't want to feel judged by you. Secretly, they want you to approach them tenderly. Not in a bullcrap kind of way–you're welcome Ones for using "crap" instead of the other word–but in a genuine gentleness.

The Eight can actually be very teachable if they respect and trust you. For Ones, who are usually natural teachers, this can be a great combination. But, it is important they build trust and rapport before this can happen. Once trust is built, Ones don't mind letting the Eight take charge–especially if the Eight leads justly.

Although Eights can bond through conflict, Ones do not.

For an Eight, it is important to voice to the One that you are on their team. The Eight's brash playful words can be internalized as a rift between them by the One. So, it is essential for an Eight to constantly reaffirm their true intentions and genuine desire for partnership with a One.

In all my relationships with Ones, I have jokingly referred to some of our disagreements as "fights." Since the Ones mean what they say, they took this very literally and seriously. Even though I used the word "fight" just for kicks, it was not helpful for the One. My uncareful use of language brought much anxiety for my One friends.

It is super important for these two to have fun together. They spend so much time deliberating ideals and decisions that they forget to enjoy one another. The Eight can help the One break out of their rigidity and the One can help the Eight recapture some of the goodness of life.

Ultimately, Ones can learn how to have fun and pursue their desires from Eights, while Eights can learn how to pursue virtue and goodness from Ones.

Twos

The Enneagram Two is called "the Helper," "the Server," or "the Encourager."

Twos are empathetic, sincere, and warm-hearted. They are also friendly, generous, and self-sacrificing, but can also be sentimental, flattering, and people-pleasing.

Well-meaning and driven to be close to others, Twos can slip into doing things for others in order to be needed. They often have problems with possessiveness and acknowledging their own needs. At times, Twos can become manipulative to get the affection they want.

At their best, Twos are unselfish, altruistic, and self-nurturing. They have unconditional love for others.

At their worst, Twos are prideful, self-deceptive, and manipulative with their love.

What We Love About Twos

Eights admire the Two's willingness to care for those who are being neglected.

Eights respect the Two's self-sacrifice to serve others.

Eights love that Two's can become a safe place for them with their care and nurture.

What We Hate About Twos

Eights are turned off by Twos when Twos try to care for them in ways that the Eight doesn't know how to receive.

Eights lose respect for Twos when they see them cater themselves to others and lose their own identity.

Eights can be triggered by the Two's expression of love, especially if it is manipulative.

How We Can Relate to Twos

These two are both the prototypical father (Eight) and mother (Two) types.

This can draw these two numbers together–the Eight and Two are the most common marriage pairing on the Enneagram–but it can also cause them issues with knowing how exactly to relate to one another. However, there is a lot of respect shared between these two numbers since they are both doers and servers.

These two numbers are also connected in the arrows of the Enneagram. The Eight takes on Two attributes when they are feeling secure. The Two takes on Eight attributes when feeling stressed. Therefore, both can learn from one another what health might look like.

Eights, as mentioned above, learned to reject nurture. Instead, Eights became the embodiment of protection.

Twos learned to reject protection and became the embodiment of nurture.

Therefore, they might both struggle to learn how to receive the very thing that the other is.

Eights can struggle with the Two's desire to care for them. This is totally understandable as the Eight is hypersensitive to manipulative love, which the Two can easily fall into when they are unhealthy. Instead of stiff arming the care that triggers them, the Eight should communicate to the Two what care they want and don't want.

In relationships with Twos, Eights need to be mindful giving the Two time to voice their thoughts. Twos are naturally averse to sharing their own thoughts and that can leave the Eight to be impatient with them and their processing.

Also, Twos can be intimidated by the vast array of opinions the Eight has. This causes the Two to be extra hesitant to share their own opinions. If you're an Eight, don't interrupt Twos after you ask them a question, they will eventually answer.

Eights can also hurt Twos by ignoring their pain and minimizing their hurt. Twos often internalize the words of the Eight, which can be a beautiful or toxic thing depending on how the Eight is using their language.

Twos usually look to powerful people and places to gauge how they're doing, and Eights can either be a force for good or evil in that regard. As an Eight, you should look for ways to affirm the Two when you see them being authentically themselves.

Eights want to see the Two respect themselves. They naturally respect Twos but can simultaneously lose respect for the Two when they see them not respecting themselves.

Twos desperately want to earn the respect of Eights but struggle to figure out how since the Eight doesn't usually praise others. This can cause a cycle where the Two tries to soften the Eight which leads to the Eight holding out. From there, the Eight will lose respect for the Two while simultaneously pushing the Two to try harder.

Overall, Twos can learn how to take charge of their own lives from Eights, while Eights can learn how to care for others in more tender ways from Twos.

Threes

The Enneagram Three is called "the Achiever," "the Performer," or "the Motivator."

Threes are self-assured, attractive, and charming. They can also be ambitious, competent, and adaptive to any social situation.

Diplomatic and poised, Threes can be overly concerned with image and what others think of them. They are status-conscious and highly driven for advancement. Threes will often have problems with workaholism and competitiveness.

At their best, Threes are self-accepting, cooperative, authentic, and everything they seem to be: role models who inspire others.

At their worst, Threes are vain, deceitful, workaholics, and have lost their identity from adapting too much.

What We Love About Threes

Eights admire the productivity of the Three.

Eights love dreaming big with Threes and talking about things on the macro level.

Eights respect the hard work of Threes.

What We Hate About Threes

Eights despise the Three's insincerity and two-facedness.

Eights look down on Threes because of how much Threes want to be liked by others.

Eights hate the Three's focus on image.

How We Can Relate to Threes

These two types can change the world when they are together. This combo gets shit done.

The Eight and Three pairing works great because Eights usually like to lead from behind whereas Threes like to lead from in front. However, both of these types' self-confidence can lead them to develop a narcissistic dynamic.

Eights can speak strength to Threes. They can remind Threes of their worth and how to set boundaries. Eights will also be one of the most loyal friends to the Three, especially when failure or scandal hit.

Threes can remind Eights of how they make others feel. This is important because Eights are normally blind to their impact on others.

Eights need to realize that the Three is actually pretty sensitive behind their professional composure. Eights should be mindful of their scowling and sharpness when engaging with Threes. Threes need to realize that Eights are more insecure than they give off and might need more affirmation than it appears.

Threes tend to see straight through the toughness and bullshit of the Eight. They don't see the value in the Eight's strength and wonder why Eights don't just get along with people like they do.

However, Threes can also be intimidated by the competence and abilities of the Eight. This can lead to the Three creating competition between themselves and the Eight. At their worst, Helen Palmer says that Threes see Eights as bullies and Eights see Threes as liars.

These two types, although extremely productive, could benefit from slowing down with one another. Instead of planning their next conference or project together, they should find some downtime and enjoy rest together.

In the end, Threes can learn how to find their true identity from Eights, while Eights can learn how to respect and value the opinions of others from Threes.

Fours

The Enneagram Four is called "the Romantic," "the Individualist," or "the Original."

Fours are self-aware, sensitive, and prone to self-isolating. They are emotionally honest, creative, and personal, but can also be moody and self-conscious.

Withholding themselves from others due to feeling vulnerable and defective, they can also feel disdainful and exempt from ordinary ways of living. Fours frequently have problems with melancholy, self-indulgence, and self-pity.

At their best, Fours are inspired and highly creative. They can renew themselves and transform their experiences.

At their worst, Fours are envious, emotionally turbulent, and self-consumed.

What We Love About Fours

Eights admire the Four's emotional intensity and willingness to express themselves.

Eights respect the Four's desire to draw near to those who are suffering.

Eights appreciate the Four's desire to be authentic.

What We Hate About Fours

Eights resent the Four's inability to get out of their own sadness and pain.

Eights despise the Four's selfishness in pursuing their own needs and desires above others.

Eights hate the Four's inaction.

How We Can Relate to Fours

There is a lot of shared love between these two types.

They both love the other's passion and intensity. They both are rebellious; with the Eight thinking they are above the law and the Four thinking they are special enough to not follow the law.

The Four admires the Eight's authenticity and in turn, the Eight admires the Four's self-expression.

Eights need to realize how they can be damaging to Fours. When Eights are raging or careless with their words, they can hurt the Four who has a deep inner sensitivity.

Fours are very feeling heavy, which can cause them to struggle with Eights who tend to want to be "right" or appear strong. Fours can also become suspicious when they come up against the Eight's emotional walls.

Fours can often feel minimized or discarded by Eights when they feel like the Eight doesn't value their opinion or feelings. Since Eights naturally view feelings as "soft" and the Four has A LOT of feelings, this can cause a tough dynamic between the two. The Four will try to stuff their feelings to fit in with Eight, but eventually will become exacerbated by not being able to voice their softer emotions.

Fours will usually need space away from the Eight but will come back to them if the Eight can approach them with their hearts rather than their strength.

Eights can speak truth to Fours about their identity and push them. They need to understand the inner wounds surrounding deficiency in the Four so they can powerfully encourage them. Since Fours are big dreamers and Eights are big doers, these two can come together to do incredible, beautiful things when they trust each other.

These pairings hit its stride when the Four's creativity and emotional intuition combine with the Eight's assertiveness and can-do attitude.

Ultimately, Fours can teach Eights how to make room for their emotions, no matter how "soft" they might appear. Eights can inspire Fours to put their creativity into action and trust themselves.

Fives

The Enneagram Five is called "the Observer," "the Investigator," or "the Expert."

Fives are analytical, insightful, and curious. They can concentrate and focus on developing complex ideas and skills.

Highly independent, innovative, and inventive, Fives can become preoccupied with their thoughts and imaginary constructs. They can become detached and high-strung. Fives also have problems with eccentricity, nihilism, and isolation.

At their best, Fives are visionary pioneers, often ahead of their time, and able to see the world in an entirely new way.

At their worst, Fives are hyperactive, scattered, and hoarders of time and energy.

What We Love About Fives

Eights admire the intelligence and expertise of the Five.

Eights respect the Five's opinions more than any other type on the Enneagram. There is a lot of built-in trust naturally from an Eight to a Five.

Eights appreciate the level-headedness of the Five.

What We Hate About Fives

Eights are frustrated by the Five's inaction. Eights can view Five's as "all brain, no action."

Eights can feel rejected by Fives when they feel like the Five chooses their own time and energy over being with the Eight.

Eights struggle with the Five's lethargy and scatteredness.

How We Can Relate to Fives

Both types are extremely logical and pursue the best answer.

They both share expertise in their fields and want their way. The Eight and Five are also connected on the Enneagram with the Eight taking on Five attributes when they are stressed and the Five taking on Eight attributes when they are secure.

Fives desperately want safety but won't tell you directly. They might just get angry for feeling unsafe and start to hunker down away from you. As an Eight, it is important to address any issues with a Five in the security of their home or safe places.

Fives are also secretly sensitive. They won't show you this and it won't show up on their bodies because they are a "head" type, but they are. As an Eight, you need to be mindful of this when interacting with them because you won't get any feedback in the moment.

Since Fives are more passive in nature, it is important to give them time and patience when talking through things. Oftentimes, Fives are unsure as to what they feel or how to express them. Don't jump the gun and tell the Five how they feel or what they should feel, even if you know you're 100% right about it.

In conjunction with this, Eights can't assume that they have figured out how a Five is going to think. Fives value being experts and Eights can frequently over assume their expertise. This will cause a Five to shut down and distance themselves from the over-opinionated Eight.

Eights have a much bigger energy supply than the Five. This can lead to conflict between the two when the Eight feels let down and the Five feels intruded upon. Because of this, Eights need to learn to acknowledge when they have demanded too much energy out of the Five.

Don't push them, the Five will pull away.

It is important to invite the Five and not demand them into things. The Five will always lean towards declining the invite to protect their energy, so it will be important for Eights to give the Five relevant information about why they should participate in the thing they're inviting them into.

The Five won't say no to you when they're exhausted, they just simply won't respond to you. This should be a good marker for Eights in learning the Five's energy supply. Eights need to learn how to control their intensity and not feel rejected when the Five gets overwhelmed.

It is helpful for Eights and Fives to exercise together. For Eights, it is helpful because they connect in their bodies. For Fives, it is helpful because they need to get more connected to their bodies.

However, as an Eight, don't expect the Five to become your lifelong workout partner. They probably won't, at least not at the level of intensity you would like.

Overall, Fives can teach Eights to pull back and learn when to not overextend themselves. Whereas Eights can teach Fives how to push their limits in healthy and constructive ways.

Sixes

The Enneagram Six is called "the Loyalist," "the Skeptic," or "the Questioner."

The Six is the only Enneagram number that has two variants within its base number: the Phobic Six and the Counterphobic Six.

The Phobic Six is a more fear based Six, while the counterphobic Six uses their fear as fuel to fight back. The counterphobic Six can often even look like an Eight!

Accordingly, there will be slightly different descriptions for each version of the Six in our below sections.

Overall, Sixes are dependable, hard-working, responsible, and trustworthy. They are excellent troubleshooters, foresee problems, and foster cooperation, but can also become defensive, evasive, and anxious. Sixes usually run on stress while complaining about it.

Naturally cautious and indecisive, Sixes can be reactive, defiant, and rebellious. They are incredibly loyal and frequently feel like their loved ones aren't as loyal to them. Sixes also have problems with self-doubt and suspicion.

At their best, Sixes are internally stable and self-reliant, courageously championing themselves and others–your most loyal friend.

At their worst, Sixes are competitive, arrogant, fearful, pessimistic, and saboteurs.

What We Love About Sixes

Eights admire the Phobic Six's loyalty and trust.

Eights respect the Counter-Phobic Six's willingness to go after abuses of power with determination and perseverance.

Eights appreciate the Six's ability to foresee potential problems and adjust accordingly.

What We Hate About Sixes

Eights resent the Phobic Six's fear and anxiety.

Eights are fearful of the Counter-Phobic Six' ability to betray and sabotage the Eight.

Eights struggle with the Six's potential irrationality when it comes to their fears and concerns.

How We Can Relate to Sixes

Sixes and Eights can usually be found together.

Whether that's working together on a project or fighting to the death over an issue, these two numbers normally find themselves near each other.

Both of these types agree on the fundamental nature of the world around them: "the world is an unsafe and dangerous place." Both scan the horizon for places or spaces of potential powerlessness. Yet, they both respond differently to these beliefs.

Eights learn to trust nobody outside of themselves to keep them safe. Sixes learn to distrust themselves and look for someone to trust to keep them safe. Eights become powerful and independent to protect themselves. Sixes make alliances to protect themselves.

Due to this, Sixes naturally find support from Eights and Eights find loyalty from Sixes. This dynamic and shared belief about the world keeps these two together.

Sixes find great comfort in the strength of an Eight. Since Eights are naturally steady, reliable, and put together, Sixes can let their guard down with Eights. They also both tend to show love through their actions, which the other appreciates greatly.

Sixes and Eights are often each other's most loyal and faithful friends. However, things can get nasty quickly if there is a breaching of trust and security between the two.

When things aren't going well, these two can have nasty fights. Both types will come into the fight thinking they're right, which generally doesn't lead to anything productive happening. These two types also tend to come at issues from completely different perspectives. Because of the Eight's dominance, Sixes might leave arguments feeling shut down or bulldozed.

It is important for Eights to listen to the Six's anxieties without judgment. They need to be patient while the Six talks and shares their doubts. Eights need to leave space for the Six to process and work through their fears without being interrupted or dismissed.

It is also helpful for Eights to use safety language with Sixes. Eights should frequently remind Sixes of their commitment to them.

Eights should also check in with the Six regularly as they might have said something minor to them that the Six's imagination has run away with. This can help the Six work through their worst-case scenarios and find security again in their relationship with the Eight.

Sixes can learn how to trust themselves from Eights, while Eights can learn how to depend on others more from Sixes.

Sevens

The Enneagram Seven is called "the Enthusiast," "the Visionary," or "the Optimist."

Sevens are extroverted, optimistic, versatile, and spontaneous. They are also playful, high-spirited, and practical. Sevens can misapply their many talents, becoming over-extended, scattered, and undisciplined.

Constantly seeking new and exciting experiences, Sevens can become distracted and exhausted by staying on the go. Sevens have problems with impatience, impulsiveness, and massive "FOMO."

At their best, Sevens focus their talents on worthwhile goals, becoming appreciative, joyous, and satisfied.

At their worst, Sevens are perfectionistic, critical, gluttonous, scattered, and undisciplined.

What We Love About Sevens

Eights admire Sevens' excitement and productivity.

Eights appreciate Sevens' hopefulness about life.

Eights enjoy the Seven's pursuit of the best things of life.

What We Hate About Sevens

Eights resent the Seven's childlikeness and overt optimism.

Eights are enraged by the Seven's unwillingness to do painful and uncomfortable things consistently.

Eights struggle with the Seven's tendency to be flaky.

How We Can Relate to Sevens

These two types are often found at the center of parties.

They both pursue energy and excitement. With the Eight's lust and the Seven's gluttony, this can be a combination of fireworks and fun–lots of fun.

In relationships with one another, Eights can learn to be more hopeful and less pessimistic, while the Seven can learn to be more grounded and stable.

Eights need to be aware that the Seven is sensitive, even when they may appear unphased. Eights usually feel heavy to Sevens when the Seven is frequently wanting lightness. This can lead to the Eight being annoyed with the Seven and pushing them even harder.

It is helpful for Eights to champion Sevens to stay in the fight. Sevens often need encouragers and cheerleaders to keep them in the rougher parts of life. Eights are great at reminding Sevens that they are stronger than they realize.

The Eight's persistence is also huge for Sevens in building their capacity for overcoming hard things, as long as the Eight remains gentle in their persistence. Even though Sevens appreciate directness, they can only handle the Eight's directness for so long.

Also, it is important for an Eight to not stay in the heaviness too long with a Seven.

It might be helpful for Eights to pick one deep issue to work through at a time because Sevens can get overwhelmed when Eights go from one heavy thing to the next. This will cause the Seven to panic and flee. Even though Sevens aren't connected to their anxiety, they will still feel the uncomfortability of back-to-back heavy conversations and try to escape.

Eights need to not take it personal when the Seven needs to tap out of the intensity the Eight brings. The Seven is not rejecting the Eight, even though it may feel like that to the Eight.

It is also important for the Seven to manage their energy levels and make sure they have a good supply when they interact with Eights. If they don't, it will lead to conflict for both of them as the Eight pushes them and the Seven pulls away to escape.

One of the most important things for an Eight in this dynamic is to manage expectations. The Seven—like the Eight—can overpromise and overcommit. Because of this, the Eight will usually feel let down by the Seven when they fall short of their commitments. The Eight should either set clear expectations with the Seven or not view their flakiness as a rejection of the Eight themselves.

Ultimately, Sevens can learn how to persevere through hardship from the Eight while the Eight can learn how to enjoy life and have more fun from the Seven.

Eights

You obviously already know everything about Eights by now.

But, just to summarize a little bit again.

At their best, Eights are self-mastering and use their strength to improve others' lives. They become heroic, magnanimous, open-hearted, caring, and inspiring.

At their worst, Eights are secretive, fearful, lustful, controlling, abrasive, and crude.

Ouch.

What We Love About Eights

Eights admire other Eights who have proven themselves.

Eights are comfortable with Eights who function as mentors or mentees.

Eights love Eights who agree with them.

What We Hate About Eights

Eights distrust other Eights who they find to be egocentric.

Eights resent other Eights who they deem to be "immature" or "unhealthy."

Eights hate Eights who disagree with them.

How We Can Relate to Other Eights

Eights either love each other or hate each other. There really is no in-between.

Between two Eights, there is normally high-volume contact. Whether it's laughing loudly, pushing the intensity to the max, or fighting like two Titans clashing, Eights interact on a grand scale.

This pairing can tend to argue a lot since conflict for Eights is often a way to connect and feel alive. For others watching two Eights interact, they might be terrified of the anger. For the Eights, it's just another day in their action-packed lives.

In the workplace, this pairing can quickly end up on a path towards destruction. With Eights frequently getting caught up in vengeance, offenses in the workplace can snowball with two Eights. The best way for two Eights to work this out is to set clear boundaries and focus on the advantages of working together.

It's super helpful for Eights to acknowledge difficulties when they are hurt. Since Eights struggle to differentiate the issue from the person causing the issue, it is important to work through these issues quickly.

If two Eights let their difficulties fester unspoken, this can lead to an all-out war. A war that might not only damage the two Eights involved but also all those around them.

As we've said before, no two Eights are the same.

Hopefully by now, you realize how complex we each are individually and how you can't just draw broad brushstrokes onto people—even though that is exactly what I did in this book.

Ultimately, Eights can learn from other Eights how to be healthier Eights. By seeing yourself in the mirror that is another Eight, Eights can learn from each other and figure out how to pursue health.

Nines

The Enneagram Nine is called "the Peacemaker," "the Mediator," or "the Harmonizer."

Nines are accepting, trusting, harmonious, conflict-avoidant, and stable. They are usually creative, optimistic, and supportive, but can also be too agreeable in order to keep the peace in their relationships.

Often wanting everything to go smoothly and without conflict, Nines can tend to be complacent, simplifying problems, and minimizing anything upsetting. They also have problems with inertia and stubbornness.

At their best, Nines are unshakable, self-developing, energetic, and all-embracing. They are able to bring people together and heal conflicts.

At their worst, Nines are anxious, worried, slothful, self-forgetting, and stuck on autopilot.

What We Love About Nines

Eights admire the safety and peace that resides in the Nine.

Eights appreciate the openness and listening ear of the Nine.

Eights trust that Nines will be there when it matters.

What We Hate About Nines

Eights hate the Nine's willingness to appease and not step on toes.

Eights resent the inaction of the Nine.

Eights struggle with the stubbornness of the Nine.

How We Can Relate to Nines

Being connected on the Enneagram through wings, these two types share a lot in common.

Outside of the Eight and Two pairing, this one might be the next most common romantic relationship on the Enneagram– with the Eight and Six pairing coming in a close third.

Nines usually admire the Eights willingness to do what is right, regardless of how those around them may feel. Nines also are inspired by the Eight's constant pursuit to better themselves and those around them.

However, this pairing has been described as when an irresistible force meets an immovable object. The Eight's strong headedness and lust for life meets the Nine's stubbornness and inertia.

If the Eight and Nine can figure out how to synthesize their two ways of relating to the world, they can become a beautiful force that moves forward. If they cannot, it will become a test of wills.

In this dynamic, it is generally extremely hard for Nines to set boundaries with Eights. If an Eight can be proactive and help the Nine set boundaries, it can do wonders for their relationship.

Both of these types tend to blame others. It will be important for an Eight to realize when they haven't been listening to the Nine rather than blaming them.

Eights can help Nines find their voice and speak up when it matters. They can also help Nines be less afraid of conflict and view conflict as an opportunity to hear someone and be heard.

Eights can also help Nines stay committed to things they believe in even when it becomes unpopular for others.

Nines can help Eights learn to not have to pick every fight. They can teach Eights how to slow down, be mindful of others, and then act. When done right, Nines can even show Eights that safety can be found through peacemaking and not just through successful conflict.

In conflict, sometimes Nines will need some space and time to gather themselves before they respond. Eights can't view this as rejection, even though the Eight would prefer to hash everything out in the moment with dramatic fashion. However, this pairing can also be great at resolving conflict since they are both logical and not "heart" types.

In a romantic context, it is helpful for this pairing to not have conflict before bed. The Eight may be able to still sleep peacefully, but the Nine might stay up all night thinking about the things they didn't say or could have said.

Overall, the Eight can learn how to lay down their swords from the Nine while the Nine can learn when and where to press in from the Eight.

As we've seen above, it is so important to approach each person with openness and humility.

We may never know why someone is the way that they are or why certain things bother them and others don't. We also may not be aware of why they make us angry or trigger us in the moment.

Because of this, it is so important that we assume the best in them and their intentions when they interact with us.

If you are still craving more on the dynamics between different types, the online *Enneagram Institute* has useful information. You can look up each different kind of pairing and find helpful descriptions.

However, what might be more helpful than anything else is to reach out to your friends and ask them how they want to be loved. Crazy idea, I know.

Just ask your friends. Ask your partner. Ask your family.

What is it they need from you? What are the things that you do that hurts them? How would they like you to speak to them? Where are the areas that you can work on to love them better?

It's that simple. You don't even need this stupid chapter. Just go ask them.

In summary, seek to be a learner of people.

Don't assume you know everything. Don't pretend that you've figured them out. Don't interrupt them when they are sharing with you.

Just listen.

Learn.

Figure out how others want to be loved and love them in that way, even if you completely disagree with it.

Just don't be a dick to people.

It's really not that hard.

CHAPTER SEVEN

I MARRIED AN EIGHT

Okay, so you married an Eight.

Did you know this going into it? How are you doing? Are you hanging in there?

I'm sure for many of you, it has been a beautiful fever dream. For others, you might be reading this book because you are at your wit's end–and that's totally understandable.

This is the reality of the Eight. We are fires that burn bright, bringing life and warmth to those around us. But, just like fires, we can also give third degree burns to those closest to us.

I commend anyone who has taken on the gauntlet of marrying or partnering with an Eight. They are not the easiest people to do life with, but when healthy, they can be some of the most beautiful people to journey with.

Whether you are married, partnered, dating, or best friends with an Eight, this chapter has helpful information for all of you. Some sections will be more geared towards Eights while others towards the loved ones of Eights.

In all of this, I find it is helpful to start with the beginning of the relationship. In this first section, we'll talk about the beginning of a romantic relationship.

This is a period that I like to call: "imprinting."

Imprinting

There's a scene in the book *Eclipse* from the Twilight Series that describes an aspect of the Eight's inner romantic life perfectly.

Jacob, one of the werewolves, describes to Bella what it's like when the werewolves "imprint" onto a partner.

"It's not like love at first sight, really. It's more like... gravity moves... suddenly. It's not the earth holding you here anymore, she does... You become whatever she needs you to be, whether that's a protector, or a lover, or a friend."

For the Eight, I have adopted this term to describe the visceral, feel-it-in-your-bones, relentless, commitment that Eights give to the partners they have chosen to love.

Imprinting is the Eight's rushing river of love that cannot be damned up. It's the tornado of affection headed straight towards their desired one. It is the unstoppable force of romantic devotion to the other.

Now, you can hate Twilight and the fact that I just quoted it in an Enneagram Eight book. That's fine.

Hate it all you want. You can burn the books and movies for all I care.

However, the "imprinting" idea rings true for most Eights I have talked to.

It's worth noting that Eights can also be little whores and jump from one partner to the next (speaking of my old self here). But, once an Eight finds that person they can trust, the imprint happens.

For Rod, an Enneagram Eight, he imprinted onto his college sweetheart Kylie, an Enneagram Four.

Rod and Kylie met when they were in college.

They were both involved in the same club on campus, even though she was a couple years older than him.

As an Eight, Rod immediately felt a connection to Kylie. He couldn't quite explain it to you, other than saying that he would do anything to be with her. As time went on, this visceral feeling burrowed deeper and deeper into his bones.

However, nothing ever happened the first couple years of knowing each other. No grand gestures of love. No dramatic moves of affection. Nothing.

As Kylie's graduation came closer, Rod knew his time was running out to make a move. So, he decided it was time. Time to make his move.

He confessed his feelings to Kylie and....

She said it wouldn't work.

She was moving a few hours away and wasn't sure if she had ever thought of him in that way. She couldn't see a future with him. She left Rod's life.

But, Rod had imprinted. He was convinced they were a good match. He knew they could make it work.

With this strong belief, Rod decided to visit a friend that Summer in the same town that Kylie lived in. He sent her a quick email saying that he would be in town and would love to see her.

Rod drove his car the few hours it took to get there, settled in at his friend's place, and dreamed about the ways he was going to win Kylie over. However, Kylie never responded to his email.

In modern terms, Kylie ghosted him.

This couldn't be the end, though. Rod had bigger plans in mind. Since they shared mutual friends, Rod knew where Kylie was living. So, he decided to stop by and pay her a visit.

"Maybe," Rod thought, "Kylie had just not seen the email yet."

Rod arrived at her place and walked up to her door. The moment was now. After a few short knocks, Kylie answered.

From there, Rod jumped into a monologue about how much he cared for Kylie and how sad he was that she ignored him. He poured his heart out and shed a few tears while explaining his love. Kylie, sensing the moment, responded with, "I will NEVER date you."

As you can imagine, Rod left dejected and depressed.

Yet, the story wasn't done.

For reasons unknown to Rod, Kylie messaged Rod later that night and said that she would explain more to him if he wanted to know why they couldn't work. Of course, Rod agreed.

This ended up being an emotional three-hour conversation where Kylie again refused to give Rod a chance. Again, Rod left dejected and depressed.

But, as fate would have it, they began emailing back and forth for the next year. Eventually, Rod told Kylie that he was starting to talk to a new girl so she needed to make up her mind about him. And as with any Enneagram Four who struggles with envy, Kylie finally agreed to date him.

With that, the rest is history. The whole nine yards. Marriage. Kids. White picket fence. Golden retriever. Love.

Okay, I lied about the Golden Retriever.

And both Kylie and Rod would tell you that their life hasn't been perfect by any standard. Rod will also tell you that you should not take any romantic advice from his story.

But, this steadfast pursuit of Kylie is very typical of Enneagram Eights. Once they imprint onto someone, it is impossible to be redirected anywhere else.

In the unhealthy versions of imprinting, an Eight can lose almost all of their autonomy. This causes extreme fear and insecurity in the Eight as they realize how dependent they've become on their imprinted person.

In healthy versions, it becomes a beautiful, committed, steadfast love towards their chosen person. They become the most loyal, passionate, and sacrificial partner a person could ask for.

I am not sure what there is to learn in this section or what might be helpful for you as an Eight, but just know that I, and other Eights, understand that visceral gut feeling you have about your partner.

We get it. We have lived it.

We understand that all-in devotion you have towards your partner. We can relate to the radical commitment you feel towards them. We know you'd take a bullet for them in the same way we'd take one for ours.

So, don't fuck it up fellow Eights. Be with that person your soul is chasing after. Stay with them.

Don't lose them because you're too damn stubborn to work on yourself. Don't make them leave you because you have refused to work on your rough edges that are pushing them away. Don't mess this up, it will be extremely painful if you do.

Speaking of fucking things up, one of the main ways Eights do this is through their fear of rejection.

Rejecting Rejection

Eights are a rejection type.

They're looking for rejection. Waiting for betrayal. They might even bait you into rejecting them.

Eights are super attuned to the negative. We are built to react very quickly to negative comments or disrespectful remarks.

In romantic relationships, Eights can tend to be overly sensitive to feelings of rejection or judgment from their partner.

Eights will tend to jump the gun on rejection. In other words, Eights will try to reject you before you can reject them.

This can show up like an Eight leaving a friendship or relationship before the other party leaves first. It might also look like an Eight assuming the worst of your critique before you even voice it to them.

This should be true for all humans, but especially don't tell an Eight "we need to talk" without any context. They will assume you are coming for a fight and will prepare their defenses for the occasion.

This is why Eights often struggle with the classic "affirmation sandwich". The "affirmation sandwich" is when someone is trying to offer a critique of you but sandwiches it with an affirmation on the front end and another on the back end. As an Eight, I will only remember the negative in the middle and not even listen to the affirmations on either side.

If anything, this makes an Eight even more closed off from affirmation because they perceive them to be shallow platitudes to lessen the blow of the upcoming critique.

Just give us the critique already.

There is also the chance that Eights will read betrayal and rejection into things that aren't either of those. Again, since they are fearful and looking for signs of betrayal, they might see betrayal in places it is not. It's important for partners to be gracious in this tendency of Eights, and for Eights to be aware of how they do this.

Obviously, nobody can be perfect when it comes to this, but this truly is the Eight's greatest fear. There will always be chances to repair as humans, but if you can be mindful of betrayal, please do it for the sake of your Eight partner. They will greatly appreciate your effort and thoughtfulness around betrayal.

For Eights, it will also be important to recognize when you get caught in self-fulfilling prophecies when it comes to rejection. We've talked about this elsewhere, but Eights can subconsciously set up scenarios where their false narratives can come out.

In other words, Eights might put themselves in situations where their close partners will inevitably have to reject them.

This might look like an Eight pushing intensity on their partner until their partner has to tap out of the conversation. Or, it might look like an Eight getting more emotional and more dramatic when they feel like they are being missed, causing their partner to detach from them, which will make the Eight feel even more misunderstood.

For Eights, we need to learn how to de-escalate and remove ourselves from these situations. Don't stack the cards against you in your relationship by constantly (subconsciously) creating scenarios where your partner will have to reject you.

I know we do this. We all do this; even other numbers do this with their different internal narratives.

For partners of Eights, you might be terrified to hurt or betray an Eight after reading this section. Don't be. If you own it and are brutally honest about it, forgiveness is there.

It's those that never own up to their betrayal that Eights struggle to truly ever forgive.

Let's talk about how we handle honesty in conflict.

Honesty Not Cruelty

Most Enneagram books will tell you that an Eight wants you to "stand up to them and be direct with them."

Although this is true in its essence, most people take this to mean "Be a total dick to your Eight partner because secretly they like it. Just trust us, we're the Enneagram experts."

Well, they're fucking wrong. Dead wrong.

We don't like it when you're mean to us. We don't like cruelty. We don't like harshness.

Granted, a playful, passionate, insult-filled fight is like heroin to us. I'm sure most Eights fantasize about getting into a dramatic fight only to end it with the best sex of their lives. We love that kind of fight.

Noah from the film "The Notebook" isn't an Eight, but the "What Do You Want" scene is an exceptionally good example of the kinds of conflict Eights like. You should stop reading right now and Google this scene to understand where I'm coming from. It is a textbook Eight fight.

Eights want honest, open, and passion-filled fighting. But, they also want their partner to come back to them. They want to make up and make love after a fight.

If make-up sex ever had a mascot, it would be Enneagram Eights.

Regardless, most Eights do not want their partners to be mean to them in a serious conversation, especially in a conversation when they show their tender heart.

The Enneagram coaches should tell you to be direct, not mean. You should be honest, not cruel. You should also be ready for the Eight to be direct and honest back.

Eights struggle with people who beat around the bush and hide what they're actually feeling from them. So, it is important and helpful for Eights when you speak clearly about what you're honestly feeling and thinking.

If you try to hide your true feelings or emotions due to your own fears, an Eight will sniff that out and internalize it like you're trying to deceive them.

Eights can sense people's hidden things: the hidden wounds, insecurities, and narratives. We can't often exactly pinpoint it, but we have a knack for knowing when someone's hiding something.

Since Eights really value inner integrity, they can feel when your outsides match your insides. We really value when someone is fully themselves and fully integrated. So, keeping things hidden from Eights is a recipe for disaster.

All that is to say, honesty is good. Directness is good. But, since most types aren't comfortable being honest or direct, this effort to be honest and direct with an Eight can often come across harsh and cruel.

If you are a partner of an Eight, learn how to use your directness and honesty in a genuine and thoughtful way.

If you are an Eight, you have to learn the same thing because you often come across too strong and harsh when conversing.

Conflict With an Eight

Another popular Enneagram expert remark is "Eights LOVE conflict."

As with many other aspects in this book, I am going to have to disagree with them. Yet again, these experts think they understand the Eight while it's abundantly clear many of them are not Eights.

Eights do not love conflict. Rather, they are just more willing to deal with conflict than other types.

For other Enneagram numbers, conflict is the bane of their existence. So, the fact that Eights seem to be okay jumping into conflict and handling it head on makes others think that Eights love conflict.

We don't.

If I could avoid conflict, I would.

The problem is that I have other values and convictions that take priority which makes conflict necessary at times.

I have found it helpful to describe the Eight's dynamic with conflict this way: for others, the idea of conflict brings them great anxiety. For Eights, the idea of conflict remaining unsettled brings them great anxiety.

I am so much more anxious when nobody is addressing the elephants in the room than I am when someone starts conflict by addressing it. I don't always love it when conflict is happening, but it's the lesser of two evils for me.

In relation to Eights and conflict, Eights will also often try to provoke others into it. Again, this might make you think it's because Eights secretly like conflict. But, no. You would be wrong again.

Eights draw others into conflict in order to find safety. For Eights, the best defense is a good offense. Withdrawal isn't safe for Eights, attacking is.

If an Eight becomes passive and withdraws, they open themselves up to the power of others to harm them. If they become aggressive and attack, they give themselves the opportunity to protect themselves.

For others, conflict can look like betrayal to them. For Eights, conflict can bring out people's authentic selves which makes the Eight feel safer. If an Eight feels someone is hiding something or holding back themselves, they might challenge or bait them into conflict to bring out what's underneath.

Eights often feel more connected after conflict because they feel like they got to see someone's true self. An Eight would rather see the ugliness underneath than live in surface level peace.

Eights genuinely want you to be your authentic and vulnerable self with them. Because of this, they will try to entice you into speaking your mind and saying what you really think and feel, oftentimes in the most raw and unfiltered language possible.

Eights love it when their partners go unfiltered to honestly say what they mean.

If you want to see your Eight get excited, tell them about a controversial opinion of yours in the most graphic, vulgar, and unfiltered language possible. Those conversations are like heaven to us. Bonus points if they already agree with that opinion too.

As Eights become older (and hopefully healthier), they might start to engage in less and less conflict, especially unnecessary conflict. As we mentioned earlier, Eights push against things to find safety. It causes more anxiety for Eights to let conflict simmer than to settle it quickly.

Yet, mature Eights have learned to find safety through other means. Since they can still feel safe even without pushing against something, they engage in less fights and arguments.

Immature Eights take every fight and meet every challenge. Mature Eights have learned to choose their battles.

In the next two sections, we'll talk about some tips for being in a close relationship with an Eight. Before we get to that, it's helpful to mention some specific tips about conflict.

If you're with an Eight, there is a good chance you have lots of conflict. Probably more conflict than you ever thought you would have with a partner.

So, here's three tips for conflict with Eights.

Conflict Tip #1 - Get to the Point.

Don't just talk and talk and talk. Eights will cut you off.

It might be hard for you to say directly what you are trying to say, but the Eight's anxiety will grow as you meander to your main point. If the Eight's anxiety grows, they will become more aggressive and harsher with you, which might blow-up the conversation.

You do not need to sugarcoat things with Eights, especially when you're talking about something other than the Eight themselves.

Keep comments brief, purposeful, and direct.

Eights are quick thinkers. They will jump ahead of you to the main point if you fluff up your comments in conflict.
Just be direct.

Conflict Tip #2 - Don't Surprise Them

As we talked about earlier with the "can we talk" prompt, Eights are always expecting the worst out of these conversations.

So, if you say "Hey, can we hangout and chat about life?" And then end up confronting them in that space about something they did or said, they will not take that nicely.

There's a good chance that if you surprise an Eight with conflict, they will lose a good amount of trust with you. Eights truly value safety in their relationships. If you abuse one of those safe places with them, it can do so much damage to the Eight's trust in you.

For many Eights, honesty from the start is super helpful. Just tell them upfront that you need to talk about the conflict itself. They won't like the fact that they have to do conflict, but they'd much rather know that going into the conversation.

With your Eight partner, you will need to figure out helpful guidelines on how to bring up conflict. Each Eight might want slightly different things when approaching conflict conversations, so it will be important to find those guidelines together. All Eights will want those guidelines clear beforehand so they can know what to expect when conflict does happen.

Overall, the more transparent, open, and honest you can be, the better.

Conflict Tip #3 - Be Prepared for Strong, Direct, and Sometimes Harsh Language Back

Unless an Eight has done a ton of work to get healthy, there is a good chance that they still don't understand how their words and actions impact you.

When an Eight is not doing well, communication can be quick, blunt, and very aggressive.

Eights are quick triggered beings. They clap back quickly.

There's no ready, aim, fire. It's just fire. Their reactions are usually an immediate response.

If you are in a conflict with an Eight, it is important for you to know that they are not always intending to come across as intense or harsh as they seem.

It is literally their body's response to feelings of unsafety.

Since Eight's are fighting types, you can normally gauge how safe they are feeling in a conversation with how harsh they are coming across.

The harsher language, the less safe the Eight feels.

It will be super important to look past the surface language of the Eight and stay in the fight with them.

There are many ways to do conflict with an Eight. Figure out the ways that work best for you.

For Eights, you also need to realize that sometimes we ask for honesty in conflict and then we get hurt by people's honesty. It is unfair to our partners to get them to do the hard work of being honest just for us to respond poorly to it.

Be better than that. Don't make them do all the work.

Eight Tips for Marriage With an Eight

There are obviously more than just eight tips for marriage with an Eight. That's just the amount I chose here.

Beyond therapy–which I recommend to anyone married to an Eight–there are countless books and podcasts to help navigate your relationship with these passionate individuals. As I've mentioned before, Helen Palmer's book *The Enneagram in Love and Work* has specific sections about the Eights' dynamics with every one of the other Enneagram numbers. Use that to help your dynamic.

Before we get into these tips, one quick note is worth mentioning: I know many of you are not married. This section is also for those who are dating, partnered, or even just best friends with an Eight. These tips work for any committed relationship.

With that said, here are eight quick tips for those who are partners (or close friends) with an Eight.

Tip #1 - Assume the Best of the Eight

If you assume the worst of the eight, you will spark their anger.

Eights usually feel misunderstood when others assume their intentions. It is much better to say, "I'm not sure if you meant it this way, but it came across this way."

Don't guess at their intent. Just ask them.

One thing I've noticed is that the word "arrogant" is a trigger word for Eights. As with any label that misunderstands Eights, this word especially activates the Eight's fight response.

They do not want to be arrogant. They are not trying to be arrogant. Even if that is how they are presenting themselves, it might be best to find another way of portraying that to the Eight rather than simply calling them "arrogant."

In terms of their intentions, Eights truly don't want to hurt those closest to them. In healthy Eights, it is devastating for them to hear how they hurt others. So, if you are feeling hurt or steamrolled by an Eight, it might be best to ask them what's underneath the aggression they're exhibiting.

Beyond this, it is helpful for an Eight's partner to seek to find out the Eight's intentions. Yes, this can be done in the moment. But, if you genuinely want to create safety for your Eight, it is best to come into conversations with their best intentions already in mind.

There's a good chance that if you're in a close relationship with an Eight, you have seen their tender, loving, and caring side. So, when an Eight unknowingly comes at you with sharp language, it is huge to keep their intentions in mind.

Eights really aren't trying to be dicks–most of the time.

Tip #2 - Stay in the Fight

You need to stay in the fight with them.

One of the best illustrations of this aspect of Eights comes from ice hockey players.

Ice hockey players will trash talk all night and get into fights on the ice. After the game, these same players might head over to the local pub and grab a beer with the person they just fought.

Eights are similar to this. They want to fight things out in the moment, and then laugh about it afterwards.

Whether that's a fight about something else or if it's literally a dispute between you two, Eights want you to stay in the fight until it is resolved or at least shelved for now. They want you to stand your ground and stick with them until the fight reaches its end. They hate avoiding conflict or leaving fights unresolved.

If you can stay in the fight, the Eight will feel more connected to you than ever. This will build trust with the Eight which will lead to them letting their tender side come out.

Tip #3 - Be Tender

When the Eight's tender heart finally comes out, hold it gently.

Now, this doesn't mean you baby an Eight at all times of the day. If anything, that will make them resent tenderness and hide their heart.

Yet, the greatest fear of the Eight is to finally expose their fragile heart to you and have you respond by ignoring or harming them.

It is helpful to view the Eight as someone with a very tender inner core that is covered up with a big shield. When that shield goes away, Eights feel extremely vulnerable and susceptible to harm. So, it is so important for partners to not mock or belittle an Eight's tender side when they finally put their shield down.

If you do belittle them, Eights will either shut down or lash out.

Tip #4 - Intentional time

Most Eights need a regular time to wind down.

Whether that's a set date night or a weekly planned "vent session," Eights need specified time to connect with you. They need a regularly scheduled time to let their energy out with you. A time where they can be their whole and true selves with you.

Eights can't just touch in every few weeks. In that scenario, Eight's tender hearts will slowly and gradually go back into hiding. If you want their true hearts to stay out in your relationship, consistent and regular check-ins do wonders for the Eight's tenderness.

Depending on their subtype, this intentional time might look different for each one.

For Self-Preservation types, this might look like working out, doing a project together, or eating at their favorite restaurant. For Social types, this might look like a game night, concert, or going to their favorite team's game. For Sexual types, this might look like a walk along the beach, talking about everything that happened that week at a coffee shop, or sex.

I guess that last one could work for all of them. Regardless, find that intentional time!

Tip #5 - Encourage Them

Eights will pretend like they don't need any affirmation or encouragement, but they actually do.

In one sense, Eights don't need a lot of encouragement. They truly do have tough skin. But, as you are aware, Eights are also deeply tender.

Eights learned at an early age to reject all outsider opinions of them in order to keep them safe, which in turn make them reject any positive affirmations of them. Because of this, Eights might have even told you that they don't need your encouragement. However, if you've gotten close enough to an Eight, you have probably seen the secret ways that they need your affirmation and validation.

Even though they are tender, this doesn't mean you lie or beat around the bush with them when there's difficult things that need to be said. They still want your honesty. But, since you are their safe person, your words also might crush them if wielded uncarefully.

Deep down, Eights want to be told they're doing a good job and that they are enough. They would like for you to acknowledge the ways that they do care and are kind. Eights are used to only being called out for their harshness and strength. They want their softer sides to be noticed too.

But, don't flatter them. They will hate it.

Tip #6 - Be Consistent

Eights need consistency.

Consistency in your words. Consistency in your actions. Consistency in your efforts.

For Eights, it will slowly shatter their trust if you tell them you're going to do something and then don't do it. For Eights, your actions are usually where they evaluate you.

If you show consistent trustworthiness, they will start to give you more and more vulnerability. If you follow-through with the things you have said, Eights will trust you deeper.

Granted, not everyone can be consistent all the time. But, if you own up to the times you aren't, Eights will forgive you.

Be someone who follows through on what they promise. The Eight will love you for it.

Tip #7 - Eights Love You Like How They Want to Be Loved

As with most humans, Eights love in the ways that they most want to be loved.

Even though this is subconscious for almost all of us, we all show love in the ways that we ourselves would like to be loved. For Eights, this gets interesting.

Eights think they're loving you by being blunt because they're not blindsiding you or betraying you. They're loving you by toughening you up and challenging you to get stronger.

Although Eights need to learn how to love better–and the next section is eight tips for Eights–it will be helpful to understand why Eights treat you in the way that they do. Sure, I know sometimes Eights are just being assholes, but other times they are genuinely trying to love you in the only ways they have learned how.

It will be important to learn how to talk to your Eight about the ways you need to be loved. It will also be important to voice the ways their "love" is being received by you, while reaffirming your best assumptions about their intentions.

Most of the time, Eights are really trying to love you. They just don't always know how to love outside of the ways they learned growing up.

Tip #8 - Let Them Be Who They Are

This one is huge.

For most of an Eight's life, they have felt like too much. They've been told they're too intense. They've been told that they overwhelm everyone around them.

Eights are beloved because of their strength and then resented when they're no longer needed. They are cherished for their passion, but then later shoved away because they are too overwhelming. People need Eights to save them from harm, and then push the Eight away once they are stable.

As their partner, as their safe person, as their person that has accepted all of them, Eights need you to champion them. They need you to call out their best and to ask them to do what they're best at.

From spouses of Eights I've talked to, many have recommended that you recognize Eights are a force of nature. They stand in the gap for you and for others. For Eights, it's an absolute joy for them to protect you and others.

So, ask them to do that for you. Ask them to be them.

Don't make them have to figure out when and where you want them or need them to be an Eight. It brings Eights so much happiness when you ask them to be strong for you. It brings the Eight joy when they can protect their people and handle conflict decisively for those they love.

Let them be them. Tell them when to be them. Don't just expect it or make them guess.

Eight's love clear and direct expectations.

Tell them what you want. They will rise to the occasion. Don't make them guess.

When Eights are being their best selves, they can be truly some of the greatest partners on the Enneagram.

Eight Tips for an Eight Who's Married

This is a book for Eights after all, right?

You didn't think I was going to let us off the hook in romantic relationships, did you?

For these next eight tips, I'll go back to using our kind of language. That's right, Bitch. We're bringing swearing back.

And yes, these tips are for more Eights than just those who are married. If you have any kind of close connection with others, these tips will be helpful for you.

Don't wait till you're married or in a long-term relationship to start giving a damn about your relationships.

Tip #1 - Slow the Fuck Down

As we've said before, we are instinct types.

This means that we often respond and react quickly. Too quickly.

You need to learn how to slow down for your partner. This will allow them to think and feel through things. They are not rejecting you or lying to you because they didn't respond immediately. They're just not an Eight.

Most people need more than a split second to determine what they think or feel about a topic. I know we have our opinions and ideas ready at the drop of a hat, but others don't.

Give them time. Give them space.

Let them respond in their time and in their way.

Tip #2 - Learn Your Impact

As Eights, we are blissfully unaware of our impact on others.

For your relationships, you should ask them what they hear when you say or do things.

How are they perceiving you? How are they hearing the words you're using? What is your body posture and language portraying that you might not be intending to? How did you come across to them?

We have to learn how to see the world through others' eyes. Our impact matters.

Often, our impact is much stronger, harder, or harsher than we are intending. Eights always need to be self-reflective in how we are impacting those around us.

Yes, our intentions matter. Go read tip #1 in the previous section. But regardless of our intentions, our impact matters just as much—if not more!

It might be helpful to ask your loved ones how they want to be loved. It doesn't matter how you THINK they should be loved. All that matters is how they receive love.

So, don't be a dickhead by just trying to love them in the way you think is best. Let them set the terms and conditions for how they receive love. Learn how you impact them.

Tip #3 - Trust Your Loved One's Words

I know that we are so strong, tough, and independent that others' words don't affect us.

However, allowing others to speak over us is actually pretty human. We're not fucking robots. We need other's words as guideposts to who we are, what the world is, and how we should see both of those.

And look, I get it. I get why we don't trust others' views. We've spent the whole book talking about this. I get it.

One year, I asked all of my friends to not even acknowledge me on my birthday.

I told them, "If I'm somehow worthy of your nice words on my birthday, then why aren't you telling me those things on other days of the year? Why is it only when you have the cultural expectation of affirmation that you now HAVE to affirm me?" It feels insincere and unnatural to me to suddenly start affirming me just because I came out of my mother's vagina on that day in the calendar.

Needless to say, birthdays are still a struggle for me. But, I have grown to learn that I need to let others' words speak to me.

Sometimes, their words are kinder and truer than my own. Sometimes, their words can speak life and goodness into me. Sometimes, we might need those words when we are really struggling.

So, let other people affirm you. I know you think they're just bullshitting you to be nice. I know you think it's fake and insincere. I know you think compliments are forced cultural niceties.

But, what would it look like if you shut that voice down and actually believed the kind things someone was saying about you? What if they're not forcing it or just saying it to be nice? What if they actually genuinely mean it, even if it is on your birthday?

I know, crazy thoughts. Just give it a shot, okay?

Tip #4 - Pick Less Fights

Do I really even need to explain this one?

You don't have to voice every counter opinion you have. You don't have to correct everyone who gets something wrong. You don't have to defend yourself every time someone disagrees with you. You don't have to address every lingering conflict to feel at peace.

You can back down in an argument once you've realized you're actually wrong. You can sit quietly and let someone else share their incorrect opinion. You can affirm and listen to people even if you disagree with 99% of what they're saying.

You don't have to fight to be safe.

Tip #5 - Give Them Space

Believe it or not, but Eights can be overwhelming for most people.

It's okay to give your partner space. It's okay to let them get time away from you. It's okay to let them sit in peace at home without drawing them into an intense conversation. It's okay to take off for a half-day and let them have the house to themselves. It's okay to just let them be.

They are not rejecting you if they need time apart from you. They are not abandoning you if they need to go hang out with other friends for a night. They are not dismissing you if they need you to shut up for a night.

They LOVE you. They WANT to be with you. They have CHOSEN to be with you.

It's perfectly normal for humans to not want to be with other humans all the time, especially the ones that they spend almost every moment with.

Just like in tip #2, learn when your partner has reached their "Eight" limit. Learn when they can't handle another deep conversation. Learn the signs of when they are exhausted and give them space and serve them without expectation.

We are NOT too much. I am not saying that. I don't believe that we are. But, sometimes we can overload our partners. It's okay to give them space. It's okay.

Tip #6 - Find Your Intensity Outlets and Emotional Regulators

We've talked about this in previous sections but it's important to mention here again: we lose our tenderness when our intensity has built up.

As an Eight, it will be wise for you to find places to let the intensity flow out of you until you get to a softer space. It will be huge to have outlets for your energy.

If anything, you can invite your partner to engage with you in the intensity outlets that they can handle.

Outside of these outlets, Eights also need interior practices to learn how to regulate their intensity. Since Eights often didn't learn the emotional stabilization practices that others did as kids, they usually need to express things in their body until they feel contained.

The only way Eights know to emotionally regulate is through expression.

Yet, there are more ways to regulate than just through intensity and expression.

Learn deep breathing practices. Join a yoga class to regulate your body. Sign up for therapy. Something other than just intensely expressing yourself with your partner every time you're stirred up.

Tip #7 - Apologize Frequently and Admit Your Errors

Boy oh boy, this is a good one.

You probably fucking hate reading this one, huh?

You might think you're already good at this one. You might even think you have very few things to truly apologize for.
I am not going to argue with you about whether or not you are right most of the time. I am also not going to argue with you about whether or not you already apologize enough.

No matter how well you think you're doing in this area, do it more. Apologize more. Admit your errors more.

Eights are notorious for not backing down. They are brilliant at winning arguments that they're actually wrong in. They are world-renowned in deflecting blame.

Don't be that way.

Learn to apologize even if you don't mean the apologies at first. Make it a discipline to continually admit the ways you were wrong. Circle back to previous arguments or fights and confess the ways you were a jerk.

Back down from arguments when you've realized you were wrong. Apologize to others after fights with them when you realize the hurtful language you used. Admit to others when you mess up.

Just do it.

Tip #8 - Let Them Be Them

Yes, I double dipped with my tips.

You got a problem with that?

If you do, then you can fuck off. Writing a book is hard shit.

Seriously, this tip is important for Eights too. We are normally even worse than our partners at letting them be them. As Eights, we push, prod, challenge, and provoke those around us to be something different than what they are.

As Eights, we need to stop this shit. People are where they are. People are who they are. People think like they do.

Yes, it might be unhealthy for them to be in the place. Yes, it might be toxic for them to behave that way. Yes, it might be immature to think that way.

Hell, they might suffer great failures and harm from you letting them be them. But, they will be okay.

As Eights, our desire to protect those closest to us–and ourselves–often leads to us not letting people walk at their own pace on their journey. It is THEIR journey after all.

We cannot expedite it for them. We cannot save them from every pitfall and error. We cannot protect them from all pain.

As partners, we need to simply be there.

Be present. Be present to their present. Be present to their current reality. Be present to their struggles. Be present to their joy. Be present to their suffering. Be present when they get hurt—and they will get hurt regardless of how hard you try to protect them.

If you haven't studied the rest of the Enneagram or your partner's number, I would recommend doing so.

This will help greatly in your understanding of why they are the way that they are.

It will help you understand why certain struggles and insecurities are hard for them. It will help you grow in empathy for them. It will show you how you can champion their strengths and goodness. It will help you let them be them.

So, just do it. Let them be them. And maybe, they'll let you be you.

There you have it. One chapter to fix your marriage to an Eight.

Pretty incredible, right? I should be a couple's therapist.

Granted, it is quite impossible to help a unique, complex relationship in one chapter–let alone in sixteen tips. But, I hope some of this has been helpful in understanding your Eight partner, as well as for Eights in understanding how they make their partners feel.

A fun practice might be to make your own eight tips. Have your partner do it too. Let each other tell you what's helpful and how best to love one another.

Regardless, the most important thing for an Enneagram Eight pairing is humility and trust.

Don't assume others' intentions. Don't keep score over each other's mistakes. Don't pretend like you have all the answers.

Trust that your partner wants the best for you. Trust that they aren't intending to hurt or betray you. Trust that any issue or problem can be worked through if you do it together.

Trust one another. Put one another first. Seek the best for one another.

Eights just want their partners and close ones to run the race of life with them. They would love to be able to look up from their race and see you running right alongside them. They want to know that you aren't going anywhere. They believe that can overcome any obstacle that comes in your path if you do it together.

Be that kind of person for an Eight. Be the person that runs the race with them.

You won't regret it.

CHAPTER EIGHT

THE PATH FORWARD

This was my hardest chapter to write.

Who the fuck am I to tell you how to be a healthy adult?

I'd much rather tell you about your past than what the path forward is. I'd much rather tell you about how we got fucked up rather than what we have to do to become whole. I'd much rather just explain why things are the way that they are.

Growth isn't easy. Change isn't easy. Health isn't easy.

The good news is that self-understanding is the first half of the journey. If you can do the deep dive of self-discovery that we started in this book, you will already be a much better human being. Yet, looking backwards is only half the journey.

We have to look forward.

This chapter is my attempt to do so for you. There will be strategies to work on. There will be things to press into. There will be areas to confront.

In this work, there are some questions we need to ask ourselves before we dive in.

Are you serious about this? Are you tired of just surviving through life and ready to thrive? Are you willing to make the necessary sacrifices and mindset changes to make this work? Are you brave enough to truly face yourself? Are you humble enough to truly see yourself–all of yourself?

If you answered no to any of this, then you can just skip to our appendix D and find some fun movies and music related to the Eight.

If you answered yes, if you truly want to find health, if you desperately want to get out of your destructive habits and patterns, if you sincerely want to be a better human, then this will take some work.

Challenging work. Excruciatingly tough work.

Yet, who are we to ever back down from something difficult?

Hard is our love language.

Before we get into all of those "how to's" of growth, there's one last part of the basics of the Enneagram we have to discuss.

I saved this section for here because it directly relates to our growth.

Stress and Security

As we mentioned earlier, the Eight is connected to two other numbers on the Enneagram when they are stressed or secure.

In other words, when an Eight is stressed or secure, they take on some of the attributes of another number. The Eight takes on negative attributes from the Enneagram Five when stressed and positive attributes from the Enneagram Two when secure.

To flesh out what these words mean, stressed doesn't just mean overloaded with work.

In this usage, stressed is feeling insecure. Stressed is feeling unsafe. Stressed is feeling unloved. Stress can mean what we usually refer to as "stress," but it can also mean so much more.

When I use stress in this section, that is what I mean.

Likewise, when I say secure, I mean the opposite of those things.

Secure is feeling safe. Secure is feeling generous. Secure is feeling loved.

Let's talk about each possibility here.

Eight to Five

No, this little section isn't about the bullshit American working hours. Don't even get me started on the lunacy of the mandated 40-hour work week.

This section is about how we take on attributes from the Enneagram Five when we are stressed, unsafe, and unloved.

For a refresher on the Enneagram Five, go back and look at our section on them in chapter 6.

In short, Fives are observant and analytical. They love to learn and become experts in their areas of interest. However, they can also become detached and hoard their energy when they are not healthy.

In our case, we generally take on the more negative attributes of the Five when we are stressed. So, that can look like an Eight hoarding energy and pulling away from others. In this stressed state, Eights become more secretive and suspicious of others.

In times of stress, Eights can start to overthink and overanalyze every situation.

When Eights are stressed, they are chronic overthinkers. Although this overthinking is mostly to the Eights detriment, it also spills out onto others too. Many Eights will use their intellect to poke holes in people and start fights when they are stressed. Eights will often viciously attack the things in others that they hate about themselves.

Eights are extremely blunt when they are stressed.

If you're an Eight, I am sure you have been in seasons—or a whole lifetime—like this.

Times when you are fearful that the world is out to get you. When you pick fights left and right because you don't trust people. When you pull away from everybody since nobody is safe. When you feel frustrated by the smallest things. When you feel overwhelmed to the point of exploding.

When people talk about Eights, this is the kind of Eight they talk about. The dictator who is constantly looking over his shoulder and destroying his enemies (and friends) before they even get a chance to negotiate peace.

As an Eight, this language of a stress-number is helpful because it can be a warning sign for us in how we are doing.

When we find ourselves becoming increasingly suspicious and distrusting of others, there is a good chance we are stressed.

When we become less generous and more antagonistic, there is a good chance we are stressed.

When we use our intellect and positions of power to bully and dominate others, there is a good chance we are stressed.

As we seek to grow healthier as adult Eights, use the markers of the stressed Five to gauge if you are stressed, insecure, or unhealthy.

Eight to Two

On the other side of this stress-security coin, you have the Enneagram Two.

Eights take on positive Two attributes when they are feeling secure, safe, and loved.

For a refresher on the Two, you can go back to chapter 6.

In short, Twos are encouraging helpers. They can be full-hearted and put the needs of others before their own. They are altruistic and heroic with their love.

Although the Two has blind spots, we will mostly be focusing on the positive since we take on positive attributes from the Two when we feel secure.

As Eights, we become more caring and compassionate when we are secure. Our heart is more open to the world and less suspicious of others. We are more connected to our feelings and engage more emotionally with people. Eights can even become way less controlling when they are secure.

When people talk about Eights, they hardly ever talk about this side of Eights.

Yes, close friends and partners might describe their Eight this way. But, the general public doesn't often see this Eight. And if they do, they probably mistype them as a Two.

If Eights pursue health, their tendency to challenge and confront will turn into encouragement and generosity. Truly, secure Eights want to lavish love and passion onto their loved ones.

When we use our hearts for justice to uplift others and care for them, we are secure.

When we connect our hearts to others, we are secure.

When we feel love and generosity exploding out of us, we are secure.

When we trust others and are willing to be hurt by them, we are secure.

As we seek to grow healthier as Eights, learn the markers of the healthy Two to gauge if you are secure, safe, and loved.

For me, the easiest way to tell the difference between when you are stressed or secure is to notice how cerebral and fearful you are versus how compassionate and empathetic you are.

Are you more in your head and more suspicious? You are probably stressed.

Are you more in your heart and more compassionate to others and yourself? You are probably secure.

Have you started to plot and plan for future fights and arguments you might get into? You are most likely stressed.

Have you started to trust others and feel those softer, deeper emotions? You are most likely secure.

There's much more that could be said about this, but these stress and security numbers will look different for each of us Eights. For you reading this, it will be important for you to find out what your own individual markers are for when you are feeling stressed and secure.

In summary, be a little self-reflective about your current state of mind and be curious about how you got in the place you are in.

Use these markers of stress and security to propel you forward.

How To Discover Your Triangles

Remember all that stuff we said earlier in chapter 3 about triangulation?

Well, there's a good chance you have developed your own triangles as an adult.

Let me explain this through two triangles.

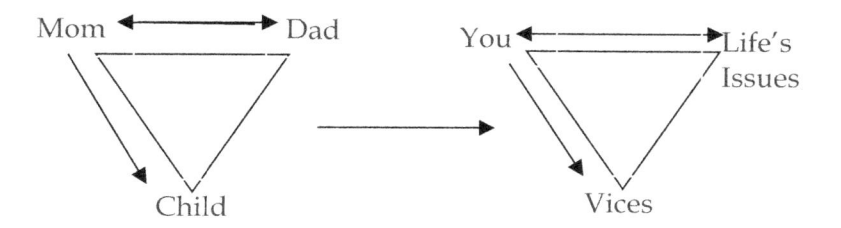

```
Mom ←————→ Dad          You ←————→ Life's
  \        /                \        / Issues
   \      /      ————→       \      /
    \    /                    \    /
     \  /                      \  /
      \/                        \/
     Child                     Vices
```

Our original triangles lead to our current triangles.

From our first triangles, we often learned unhealthy narratives about what emotions were okay and not okay. We might have also learned unhealthy coping mechanisms from those original triangles. We might even avoid and elude life's issues in the same ways our parents did.

In this journey of health, we often can't even come close to starting the work because our vices get in the way. We can't even start to look underneath the surface at our negative narratives because we are numbing ourselves with our coping mechanisms. In this way, we create new triangles and don't deal with our current issues like our parents before us.

In other words, let me give you a real-life example of a triangle from my life.

In my younger years, I grew up in a relatively conservative Christian environment.

Because of that, sex and sexuality were not something regularly talked about. Pornography was especially not talked about.

Great idea, right?

Due to my luck, I actually first stumbled upon pornography in Halo 3.

For those nerds out there, Halo 3 had this "file sharing" option where you could share your cool clips or maps you made. In this instance, I saw someone title a clip called "sick overkill."

As a young 6th grader, I had to see this awesome play.

To my surprise, the file was actually a picture of Kim Kardashian almost fully nude.

This was my first exposure to naked things and the hold they have on a young man.

It wasn't until years later that pornography became a more regular thing in my life.

As I got older and more emotionally detached from my family, porn became my outlet.

It became something I turned to when I was sad. It became something I looked at when I was stressed. It became something I consumed when I was anxious.

Although I didn't realize it at the time, porn became the thing I used to comfort and distract myself from my own life's issues. Porn was a place where I could turn away from my current emotional realities.

Porn became a part of my triangle.

Now, some of you may have different views on pornography and its values or vices. I am not here to make a broad brushstroke on explicit media, but simply my own experience.

For me, pornography became the thing I used to avoid my real-life problems–which is exactly what a triangle does.

Instead of dealing with my deeply held feelings of rejection, I watched porn.

Instead of finding safe places to regulate my anxiety, I looked at naked things online.

Instead of processing my abandonment, I found acceptance by women on my screen.

This is what triangles do. They keep you from dealing with the real-life issues that you are facing. They keep you stuck in a cycle of never truly moving on from things.

For you, your part of the triangle might be alcohol. It could be drugs. It could be video games. It could be binge eating. It could be social media and entertainment. It could be chronic relationships or hookups.

It could be literally anything you are using to avoid dealing with the deeper issues at hand.

For you Eights, it will be huge to identify these.

What do you turn to in the hours after an emotionally exhausting conversation? Where do you go when you feel sad, angry, or anxious? Is that outlet helping you process these emotions or making you avoid them entirely?

Some of your outlets might be healthy, normal, and good for you. Most of them are probably not.

We can never truly deal with the real shit of our lives and our internal worlds if we're numbing ourselves in our triangles. We have to remove our comforts and distractions from our triangles in order to truly process those issues.

For you, this might be the biggest and hardest first step. I know it was for me.

We have developed dependencies on these things. It will be tough to get off of them.

But, if you genuinely want to open yourself up to joy, you need to get at the deeply held beliefs and things that are keeping you from it. In order to get under the surface, we need to remove the vices that keep us from dealing with them.

Once we deal with our triangles, we can start our work.

How to Be Vulnerable

Why is vulnerability put forward as a virtue?

Why are we all just assuming that this is a good thing to get in touch with our vulnerability?

What if the Enneagram experts are just a bunch of soft bitches?

Great questions. I've asked these myself many times.

The reason we pursue vulnerability is because it allows us to finally experience love.

It's that simple.

When we are vulnerable, when we are tender, when we are exposed, we are actually in the perfect position to finally experience true love.

If we protect ourselves, if we guard our hearts, if we build fortresses around us, we cannot experience love.

Love requires vulnerability. Love requires risk. Love requires the potential of harm.

You cannot be loved by someone if you cannot be harmed by them.

I wish this weren't true, but it is.

This is why most Eights have a passionate and fierce love for their romantic partners. They have finally experienced some of this "true love" with them. This is also why Eights are hurt by their romantic partners more than anyone else.

Indeed, the only way to experience deep, genuine, life-changing love is to open yourself up to someone who can harm or even betray you.

If you are still not convinced, that's fine.

You can live in your fortified fortress for the rest of your life. It might keep you safe. It might keep you free from deep harm. It might keep you protected from betrayal.

But, it will not be a place of love.

Becoming vulnerable will be uncomfortable. It will be awkward. It will be unnatural for us.

In many ways, it will look like using your non-dominant hand. For me, becoming vulnerable felt like shooting jump shots with my left hand. It felt like doing basic tasks but with uncoordinated and uncalibrated movements.

The true way to practice vulnerability is going to feel backwards. It will feel like falling backwards. It will feel like going backwards in your growth journey.

Sometimes, you have to get worse before you can get better. This is true of vulnerability as well.

In order to not smash the vulnerability hammer over your head repeatedly, we will move forward. In these next sections, we will focus on three areas that will help you in your journey towards growth as an Eight in vulnerability.

Intensity outlets, weaknesses, and limits.

Use Your Intensity Outlets

One of the primary ways an Eight can get in touch with their vulnerability is to find intensity outlets.

These are places where the Eight drains their body of their energy and intensity so that their softer, gentler hearts can come to the surface.

Generally, you can determine an Eight's level of health by how unrelentingly intense they are.

Now, this doesn't mean that if an Eight is intense, they are unhealthy. Don't twist my words and use it against Eights.

But, if an Eight is unrelenting in their intensity, then that might be a good gauge about their level of health.

For example, if an Eight is jumping from one intense thing to the next, and then comes home and immediately starts a fight with their partner, there is a good chance they are not doing well.

The reason for this is that Eights' bodies are covering their hearts. Their bodies are felt before their hearts. Their bodies don't allow their hearts to come through.

An Eight's intensity outlet might look like working out. Not just any workout, but a good one-to-two-hour workout with multiple layers of exercise or intensity involved.

This could be a full body workout, CrossFit, or a 30-mile bike ride going uphill both ways.

Other Eight's intensity outlets might look like grabbing coffee with their other intense friend to have an intense conversation. This could be a conversation about the latest political drama. It could be a conversation about their specific field of work and the struggles therein. The conversation could be about literally anything as long as they are intense, raw, and honest.

For some Eights, their intensity outlets look like quitting their desk job to work in a field of justice. This way, they are guaranteed 40 hours of intense justice pursuits.

Finally, for many Eights, it could look just like doing normal things in intense fashion.

This could look like eating until they are about to throw up.

It could look like having sex multiple times in one day, pursuing pleasure and fun to the highest degree each time.

It could look like playing video games for 6 hours straight on their day off.

It could look like spending all afternoon doing their favorite hobby or interest.

Literally, just take any normal thing you like to do, and do it harder.

These outlets are essential. If we don't have them, things can get nasty. If an Eight doesn't have intensity outlets, they will inject intensity into places they truly don't belong.

Eights without intensity outlets can cause many problems and issues with those closest to them. They can turn ordinary situations into extreme and intense ones.

Oh, you have a fun dinner date planned with your Eight partner? Have fun talking about the effectiveness of gun control being stifled by the corruption and hypocrisy of politicians.

Oh, you went out on a casual hike with your Eight friend? Have fun running up the mountain until you're on the verge of puking.

Oh, you wanted to catch up with your Eight colleague over lunch? Have fun hearing about how much of an asshole your boss is and how the whole company is incompetent.

Oh, you wanted to discuss recent events with your Eight parent? Have fun ending up in an intense argument and inevitably losing because your parent refuses to back down.

Oh, you wanted to talk about chores with your Eight roommate? Have fun being exposed for every little quirk and uncleanly thing you do.

I could go on and on with all the ways an Eight lives into the stereotype of being an Eight. When Eights don't have intensity outlets, they truly live up to the worst parts of themselves.

They bully those around them. They are brash and harsh with their words. They turn light conversations into heated ones.

As an Eight, if you can catch yourself before you do this, you will do wonders for the health of your relationships.

If you feel on the verge of yelling at someone because you think they're lying, breathe.

If you feel the sudden urge to disagree with someone for no damn reason, slow down.

If you feel the incessant need to correct someone who said something wrong, hold it in.

Yes, people lie. Yes, people have stupid opinions. Yes, people are bumbling idiots. But, that doesn't mean you need to address it every damn time.

You can let someone lie. You can allow someone to voice their incorrect opinion without chiming in. You can hold your tongue when someone messes up.

If you can find places to allow your intensity to flow, you be far more gracious to everyone around you–including yourself.

Dare I say, you might even be a more honest and authentic version of yourself?

As Eights, we cannot get in touch with our vulnerable sides unless we get our intensity out. Vulnerability and intensity can often not coexist–I guess unless you are intensely vulnerable.

The intensity needs to be removed so the more vulnerable parts of us can come forward.

Once we get our intensity out, we usually become aware of some of our weaknesses.

Embrace Your Weakness

Sure, I bet you already know some of your weaknesses.

You might be able to admit you're not good at encouragement. You can confess that you suck at tennis but it's a "pussy sport anyway" so you don't really care. You might even be able to identify that sometimes you're "too rough."

However, embracing your weaknesses is more than just a mental affirmation of some deficiency.

We have to truly wear our weaknesses. We have to let them speak to us without dismissing them. We have to include our weaknesses as a part of our being and not this secondary attribute that exists outside of us.

We are our weaknesses. We are our weaknesses just as much as we are our strengths.

If anything, our weaknesses are what makes us human. I know it doesn't seem like it, but that's actually a good thing.

So, how the hell do we embrace things that we don't truly know? How can we actually believe the words of others when they expose our weaknesses? How do we embrace weakness?

My first recommendation would be to let others tell you them.

Full stop.

For me, I practiced embracing my weaknesses through a super fun exercise in my 20's.

I reached out to 30 of my closest friends, peers, and colleagues and asked them each a simple question: "What do you think are my strengths and weaknesses?"

From here, I went and wrote down my own answer to that question. This way, I could compare my perception of self with everyone else's.

As their responses came in, I put them into a huge document. I would clump answers together and note specific strengths or weaknesses that multiple people answered.

Then, I just sat in it. I sat in anger from feeling betrayed by some of the responses. I sat in their honest views of me.

It was excruciating.

I felt seen at times. I felt misunderstood by others. In all, I felt exposed.

Now, you don't have to do this exact exercise, but you damn well need to do something similar.

One of the biggest flaws in the Eight is rooted in one of our strengths. We have the beautiful strength of being able to carve out our own identity–remember how Eights think: "I don't give a shit about what others think, I only care about what I think."

Yet, that strength also leads to one of our biggest weaknesses. We have no idea how we are perceived by others. We have no idea how they view us. We dismiss their opinions of us, which leads us to missing their clear perspective of our blind spots.

We CANNOT grow, heal, or work on ourselves if we do not let others speak into our lives. We must open ourselves up to their feedback. We must let them tell us the truths of who we are.

Remember above how I asked if you were willing to do hard shit to grow? This is one of those.

Be willing to let others tell you their experience of you.

Listen to them and believe their words about you.

Embrace your weaknesses.

Learn that you can still be safe even if you feel small.

Real strength is found through facing your weaknesses.

This is true vulnerability.

Learn Your Limits

Vulnerability can also be accessed through your limits.

As we mentioned above in our discussion on vulnerability, vulnerability is experiencing the current possibility of being harmed emotionally or physically. It is submitting yourself to the limits of your own protection.

It is in our limits that we can be vulnerable. It is in our limits that we can find true connection to others.

As Eights, we often believe things like "I'm the only one who can lead, do what's necessary, and perform the duty at hand."

Although this might be true in certain situations, this thinking leaves us alone and disconnected. When we believe that nobody can help us or that we are only capable of a task, we isolate ourselves from their help and care.

I find that we do this because we often refuse to admit our limits.

Let me explain with a story from the time period around John's suicide that I mentioned earlier in chapter 4.

I never experienced the harm of going past my limits until the night of John's death.

My body told me to not go in that room alone. My brain wanted to admit to my friends that I was terrified. My heart wanted to be held by my Dad or Mom and saved from that situation.

But, I couldn't admit those things. I couldn't admit them to myself. I definitely couldn't admit them to my friends that night.

I had to deny they existed.

I had to protect my friends. I had to save the day. I had to do the thing that nobody else could do.

From that thinking, I went past my limits. My body collapsed within. My brain cracked. My heart shattered.

After that night, it started a stretch of 4 months of panic attacks.

I would have panic attacks while sitting alone in my room. Panic attacks from taking the dog for a walk. Panic attacks from performing the most basic human tasks.

By going past my limits, my body, mind, and heart were all in chaos.

Yet, there was beauty in this season too. There was beauty in having limits. There was beauty in needing others' help.

I cannot tell you how many times I had to call my friends and have them drive over to sit with me while my body convulsed with panic. The many times I had to cancel plans because I was having another panic attack. The many times I had to have friends and loved ones perform simple tasks for me because I wasn't functioning.

I went from having no limits to having no capacity. I was utterly helpless. I was completely dependent on my loved ones.

I absolutely hated it.

It felt like I had to die a million deaths. I had to be a burden on others, which was hell for me. Admitting my true helplessness was literal torture. It was almost worse than the panic attacks themselves.

In the weird paradox of the universe, this time was also the most loved I have ever felt. The most connected I have ever been to my friends. The most accepted I have ever been.

I found deep acceptance and belonging when I had to depend on my friends and loved ones. I found true love when I finally embraced my true limits and needs.

For you, I hope you can learn the beauty of limits in a less dire way.

I hope it doesn't take panic attacks and curling up in the fetal position for you to depend on others. Learn from my story.

Love can be discovered in our limits. We are so used to being admired and accepted for our strengths but we are terrified of acknowledging our limits.

I'm sure we have many insecurities about embracing this.

What if nobody wants the weak version of me? What if my friend's won't want me around if I can't be as strong as they have known me to be? Will I be rejected if I become a burden on people?

If you have good people around you, I can promise you that embracing your limits and depending on others is the greatest thing you can do. Learning to be loved in your limits is truly learning love itself.

Find those people to practice your limits with. Don't wait until your life comes crashing down to start acknowledging that you are not all-powerful.

Please. Don't wait till you crash. It's not worth it.

It will be important for you to find places where you can be vulnerable.

You will need to find intensity outlets, so that you can discover your weaknesses and learn your limits. Once you have done these, you might finally see your true vulnerable self.

It is in this vulnerable self that you can experience the love your life has been looking for.

This will be hard, but it will be worth it. You need to find places where you are open to being attacked. True vulnerability requires this reality. It is only in that condition can you experience genuine intimacy with another.

You have to open yourself up to the potential of pain in order to experience the depth of connection. You have to put yourself in harm's way in order to find yourself in love's arms. You have to be vulnerable to be loved.

Pursue vulnerability.

How to Handle Betrayal

Since you are a human being reading this, there is a good chance you will experience betrayal in your life.

As Eights, we wish this wasn't the case. We wish that everyone could just tell the truth. That nobody would deceive you. That people would play fair in the game of life.

Unfortunately, that is not the reality.

So, how do we deal with betrayal? How do we relearn how to trust others when they betray us? What is the pathway towards being able to withstand those moments of betrayal?

This section will attempt to cover that.

Betrayal Loop

Before we talk about how to handle it, it is important to note how we end up in situations of betrayal.

Yes, sometimes we put ourselves in positions to be betrayed. Sometimes, the human psyche creates self-fulfilling prophecies. In our case, we do that with betrayal.

Our betrayal loop looks like this.

Let's imagine you are an Eight.

You believe the world is dangerous and that people aren't safe. Yet, somehow you still become close friends with a person.

This is great right? Eights love having people to trust.

But, as you tend to do, sometimes you demand too much of your friend or become too blunt and aggressive with them.

Since most people can't handle this, your friend pulls away from you. Once they pull away, you start to feel abandoned and betrayed by them.

Since Eights are fighters when faced with fear or pain, you start to push your friend even harder and become even more aggressive with them. When this happens, your friend pulls away even further.

With this, you feel even more betrayed.

We could keep going and going with this cycle. Just follow the pattern until its logical end of the Eight going on a rampage against those who they once loved.

This is the betrayal loop.

A loop we find ourselves in often. A loop that when you get caught in, can get nasty very quickly.

It's essential for Eights to recognize when they've gotten themselves in situations like this. If they can realize it once they are in it, they can hopefully back down before it gets worse.

In some ways, it's like when your dog gets off the leash.

When a dog gets off the leash, they generally run wild. In most cases, no matter how much you raise your voice or chase after them, they will just keep running away from you. So, dog trainers advise that instead of continuing your pursuit of them, you simply sit on the ground and wait for the dog to come back to you.

In the same way, when we realize our friends might be pulling away due to our aggressive demeanor, we must back down. I know everything in our being says to push harder and pursue them stronger, but that will most likely make them pull away even more.

We must learn to back down in situations like this. We must learn to allow others to gradually come back to us and not run them out of our lives. We must learn that their need for space isn't betrayal or abandonment.

If we don't learn this, we will perpetually feel misunderstood, abandoned, and betrayed. In this state of mind, it will be impossible to overcome betrayal.

Overcoming Betrayal

For Eights, betrayal is an ever-looming possibility.

Although that sounds dramatic, it's true. We learned this. We learned the world would leave you, deceive you, and betray you.

The work of the Eight will be to unlearn those narratives and learn new ones.

This is hard work. But, it's work we must do.

For Eights, their child-self learned betrayal. Instead, they needed to hear, "It's okay to be vulnerable and trust others. You will not be betrayed."

What would it be like to believe that positive narrative over the idea that the world is out to get you? What if we chose to believe that our friends were not intending to hurt us even when they did? What if we looked at the world as a place of acceptance and safety rather than rejection and harm?

On page 301 of one of my favorite fantasy novels, *Mistborn*, there's a scene that's helpful to quote here. Kelsier and Vin, the two main characters, get into a heated conversation about betrayal.

"*'Do you stop loving someone just because they betray you? I don't think so. That's what makes the betrayal hurt so much—pain, frustration, anger... and I still loved her. I still do'*

'How?' Vin asked. 'How can you? And, how can you possibly trust people? Didn't you learn from what she did to you?'

Kelsier shrugged. "I think given the choice between loving Mare—betrayal included—and never knowing her, I'd choose love.

I risked, and I lost, but the risk was still worth it. It's the same with my friends... I'd rather trust my men than worry about what will happen if they turn on me.'"

Kelsier's words here speak to us Eights.

Which reality do we want to live in? Suspicion, defensiveness, and distrust of those closest to us? Or hope, trust, and love?

We get to determine how we view the world. We can view it through a lens of betrayal or we can view it through a lens of love—which makes every betrayal worth it, no matter how painful.

I wish there was an easy 12-step program to solve betrayal in your life. I desperately wish that this work was a linear process. Yet, as you have seen in this chapter, there aren't many programs for our problems.

This work will be a work of healing past wounds. It will be a work of changing your perceptions and narratives. It will be the challenging work of trusting others again.

The most important thing an Eight can do for betrayal is to find close people that they can trust with their whole being.

In these secure relationships, Eights need to practice reinterpreting your friend's harms against you as a reality of life and not as betrayal. Eights need to trust that they can recover even when they are genuinely betrayed by their friends. Eights need to choose to believe that their friends love them.

Betrayal doesn't have to be the end. It doesn't have to be the end of friendships. It doesn't have to be the end of partnerships.

Betrayal can be just that: betrayal.

A painful, hurtful, blindsiding pain. But, pain is not the end. Hurt is not the end. Betrayal is not the end.

I honestly believe that Eights can learn to recover from betrayal. Eights can also learn to not internalize minor offenses as betrayal. Above all, Eights can learn to trust others again–even if it starts with a few people, maybe even just one.

To close this little subsection, I'll leave you with a simple question to gauge how you have grown with betrayal. If you can answer yes to this question, then you have done some work in overcoming betrayal.

Do you have people in your life that can hurt you?

If the answer is no, that's okay. The journey now begins to find those people.

How to Befriend Your Inner Child

I know this sounds soft, but hopefully you've gotten over that by now.

This might be the most important thing you can do in your Eight journey.

Some believe that if they can just ignore their child self and deny those painful memories then they will be fine. They think that since they are no longer that 12-year-old boy or 8-year-old girl, then those narratives no longer affect them. They're a grown ass adult now, not some stupid little kid.

This doesn't work.

If you completely deny your child self and shut them up, they will still subconsciously influence into your decisions, actions, and beliefs. I'm sorry, but that's just how it goes. Ask any psychologist.

We have to take our healthy adult selves to our child selves. We have to use the maturity, wisdom, and safety of our adult selves to pick away at some of the wounds and insecurities of our child selves. We have to become the safe and secure parent that our child self desperately needed.

I am convinced that so many of our negative behaviors, thinking patterns, or emotional outbursts are connected to unprocessed wounds, memories, or narratives. If you truly want to become a better human being, you have to engage your younger self.

In that season I mentioned earlier where my good friend committed suicide, I spent a lot of time with my younger self. It seemed like he had come to the forefront and was controlling my adult life again even though it had been years since he had come out of hiding.

My adult-self that protected my child-self collapsed. This scared, shy, fearful, and lonely child was now dominating my decisions and everyday life. With that, my child-self was left exposed. It was truly terrifying.

My demeanor changed. My confidence was gone. My body posture even resembled that of a child.

I started eating some of my favorite childhood snacks (bagel bites and apple cinnamon rice cakes). I started playing some of my favorite childhood games (Halo). I started doing puzzles to engage my mind away from the horror that existed outside.

I had to relearn how to be an adult. I had to learn how to comfort that kid and let him exist. I had to learn how to let both my adult-self and child-self coexist. I had to learn how to regain confidence.

I had to relearn how to trust the world again.

One of the most impactful things I did was write myself a letter. From the adult-me to the child-me. I did this to bring harmony and unity between my strong adult-self and my innocent-child.

I wanted to share this letter here to inspire you to do the same and to start that conversation with your younger self.

Reading this letter now brings me tears. It was such a journey to bring my adult-self and child-self into harmony. I hope it blesses you like it did me.

Here is my letter:

Dear Coco,

I know you're scared. I understand your pain. I can feel your fear.

It all makes sense. Your anxiety and fears are real. Your insecurities are screaming at you. They feel like they will be here forever. The world seems so incredibly scary.

I know you feel alone, very alone. I know you feel like you have nobody to turn to, to go to, to run to. I know you feel like there's no place to take your pain and fears.

I know you're shy. I know you're uncomfortable with your body and interacting with girls. I know you dread having any kind of attention on you, especially from crowds.

I know you desperately want friends like your older brother has. I know you desperately want the confidence like your older sister has. I know you want your mom and dad to stop fighting. I know you want your siblings to stop picking on you. I know you want them to stop calling you those terrible names.

I know you're scared of your parents finding out about your secrets. I know you feel ashamed and confused about many things. I know you would rather hide than be exposed.

I know there's so many things you fear and are scared of. I know there's so many things you feel alone and isolated in. I know there's so many things you are ashamed of.
I've experienced all of this too.

I remember those moments. I remember that pain. I remember that feeling of loneliness and isolation. I remember feeling helpless. Utterly helpless.

I remember when you were 4 and got accidentally burned by an iron landing on your arm and the pain you felt. I remember when your mom pulled your pants down in front of her friends to show them how tan your butt was and how ashamed and used you felt. I remember your siblings telling you that you were adopted, slow, and fat until you cried. I remember the time your older brother and cousin mocked you until you cried and hid in the bathroom, and then they mocked your crying. I remember your sister hitting you repeatedly and then getting you in trouble when you hit her back. I remember your brother keeping you up late at night competing against you in games until he won and then sending you to bed with a loss and tears. I remember the many days and nights you had to compete against your brother's older friends and the emotional and physical toll that secretly took on you. I remember the many times the only friends you had were your dogs.

I remember when you were 8 and you were so afraid of playing in a basketball game that you almost threw up. I remember the ever-present awareness that you were on the outside looking in on your family. I remember the many times you played alone because you were homeschooled. I remember your coaches pushing you beyond the limits of what a 12-year-old could stand. I remember mom catching you touching yourself and telling you that dad was going to talk with you about it, and then he never did. I remember the turmoil of home just as you were hitting your teenage years. I remember when you would get called on in youth groups and you would blush so much that you started to sweat. I remember your guilt for discovering porn at a young age and having nobody to talk to. I remember when you used to hide in your room with anxiety worrying about if your mom and dad's marriage was going to make it.

I remember when you were 16 and you used to drive alone at night to the spots of your painful memories to cry while you relived them. I remember the overwhelming pressure you felt to excel at sports, school, and in relationships. I remember the pain you felt that night on the basketball court alone when Dad didn't come out. I remember the night your girlfriend cheated on you and it felt like your heart was caving in. I remember the agony of losing all your friends in High School and your girlfriend due to your faith. I remember that first panic attack you had two days before college started.

I remember the many, many, many times you cried alone. I remember all the pain, hurt, and betrayal you had to endure. I remember that ever present feeling of being alone, scared, and helpless.

I remember.

I don't remember all of it but I remember enough to say that I see you. I see all of you, Coco.

But in all of this, you made it. I made it. We made it.

We faced down those fears and showed them to be not as scary as we thought. We faced our loneliness and made friends and new family. We faced our shame and found acceptance, forgiveness, and understanding.

We've become secure in ourselves and can withstand any insult that comes our way. We grew into our bodies and developed them in healthy ways. We found ourselves outside of our family and developed an identity, purpose, and personality. We've led friend groups and sports teams. We've won girls over and dated them. We've spoken in front of crowds of 10's, 100's, and 1000's. We moved to a whole new city two times, survived, and even thrived. We've found new fathers, mothers, brothers, and sisters. We've learned to take care of ourselves and others and found those who can do the same.

I am, we are, an example that the fears aren't as lethal as we think, the insults don't last as long as they can hurt, the alone periods are much shorter than the times of belonging, the moments of shame are dim compared to the moments of acceptance, the moments of abandonment are brief compared to the moments of love, and that the light of life is breaking into the darkness of your current reality. And, that light is bright. Beautifully bright.

You, I, we can do it, kid. We have done it before and we can do it again. We will do it again.

This time, we won't have to do it ourselves. We've surrounded ourselves with so many to help. We are going to be okay.

We're going to be more than okay.

*Love,
C.V.*

You may not choose to write a letter to your younger self. You may not choose to recount all of the things that happened to you and the narratives you learned because of it.

But please, I beg you. Do some kind of work that softens you up. Do something that makes you more compassionate towards yourself and others. Do something that's honest, open, and vulnerable.

Engage your "Switch" story. Talk with someone safe about the abuse, neglect, or trauma you experienced. Embrace that scared, powerless, and helpless child within you.

Jump into the abyss of your childhood. Dive headfirst into your trauma. Swim in the waters of broken promises and failures.

Do the hard, scary, and intimidating work of engaging your deeply held wounds and narratives. Heal those wounds. Change those narratives.

And, don't do it alone. Take safe people with you on the journey.

You can do it. We can do it.

Here we are. At the end of the book.

What have we learned? What has brought us direction? What has pissed us off?

I'm sure you might have been expecting more out of this final chapter. Some great metaphor, story, or discipline that you can implement tomorrow in your life to become a better person. I'm sure you picked this book up with hopes of it fixing how much of an asshole you are.

It's truly hard to close this chapter. There are not simple fixes to complex human realities. There's not a magic solution to being an Eight. I can't tell you exactly what to do to become healthy.

I don't know your story. I don't know your pain. I don't know your false narratives.

However, I would imagine there's some that do. Maybe it's your spouse. Maybe it's a parent or sibling. Maybe it's just one singular friend.

The best advice I can give you is to invite them in. Let them see those wounds. Let them hear your stories. Let them experience your pain.

With those people, discover your individual path ahead towards health. Let them join you on that journey. This work is so much easier and more fruitful when we don't do it alone.

However, if you're still wanting more directives than what I have given above, I have included a whole appendix with 88 imperatives for Eights to do to grow. You're welcome.

Yet, we must close this book. If you've made it this far with an open and humble heart, I applaud you.

It's hard as shit to hear the truth about us. It's hard as hell to look at our naked ass selves in the mirror and notice all that we are. It's hard to heal, grow, and be a healthy adult.

This work is fucking hard.

But, who better to do this hard work than the most badass number on the whole Enneagram?

I truly believe that if Eights can take their tenacity, fearlessness, and perseverance to their emotional health, then they can become remarkable human beings.

If Eights can take their courage, strength, and boldness to the realm of their insecurities, failures, and false narratives, then they can transform themselves. If Eights can take their intensity and put it towards growth, then they can become incredible people. If Eights can challenge themselves to go deeper, then they can discover love and joy.

All of the tools we have learned from our failures and betrayals, we can now use to heal those very things. We have everything we need to be able to start this work.

I've thought of all the ways to end this book. I have thought of snappy one liners and heroic stories to close it. I have thought of tying together this work into a nice little bow. All of those might have been a great way to end this book.

The journey ahead isn't flashy. It cannot be summarized in a one sentence quote about life. It cannot be captured in a single story.

I cannot tell you nor promise you that the days ahead will be all worth it. I cannot promise you that the work towards health and growth as an Eight will always be rewarding. I cannot promise you that your growth will be linear and gradual.

You will probably fail at this. You will probably give up at times. You will probably feel like you're worse than you started. You will probably feel the overwhelming weight of life and its consequences. You will probably feel like reverting back to your old ways at every stop on the way.

Doing this inner work might feel like a wildfire has ravaged through your internal world's forest. There might be hardly anything left that keeps you stable. There might be just ash and devastation.

Yet, just as with any wildfire, the soil that remains after is the most fertile soil the earth has to offer. That inner soil can be the place where you see new patterns, habits, and beauty arise. That inner soil can be the place that you finally break free from all those unhealthy patterns, behaviors, and narratives you have. That inner soil can be the place where you truly grow into the person you've always wanted to be.

And maybe, just maybe, you will start to see new and beautiful flowers sprouting up in that forest.

Yes, I just ended this Enneagram Eight book with a fucking flower.

Deal with it.

APPENDIX A

QUESTIONS FOR EIGHTS

Here are some questions to reflect on that match each chapter's content.

These are 5 questions you can ask yourself if you are an Eight or questions that you can ask your Eight friends and partners.

I would have included these at the end of each chapter, but as an Eight, I always hated books that did that. Just give me the content. I don't want to be all soft and reflective.

Regardless, I included them here. Use them or don't. I don't care.

Chapter 1

1. What resonated with you the most about the Eight description? What do you feel like doesn't fit you?
2. How do people misunderstand you and your motivations?
3. Do you feel like you have fears? How do they play out in your life?
4. What has protection looked like for you? Do you feel like you have people who you can turn to?
5. Is vulnerability hard for you? Do you feel like you have safe people that you can be weak with?

Chapter 2
1. What do you think your wing is?
2. Do you feel like you have different wings in different contexts?
3. What do you think your dominant subtype is? How does that show up in your life?
4. What do you think your repressed subtype is? Where can you see that repression?
5. If you are a female Eight, what has your Eightness looked like? How have you learned to be who you are in our society?

Chapter 3
1. How would you describe your childhood-self? What were they like?
2. When was your switch? Was it one moment or many? Can you think back to when you last identified as a kid?
3. Do you feel like you lost your innocence in childhood too fast? Have there been any ways where you have tried to recapture it?
4. Were you in any triangles growing up? What did those teach you about yourself and the world around you?
5. What has sadness and sorrow looked like in you? Do you find it hard to express those kinds of softer emotions?

Chapter 4
1. What has your relationship been like with your body? Do you feel it has been negative or positive overall?
2. Do you resonate with the "sadness to anger to energy renewal cycle"? How has anger protected your other softer emotions?

3. Where do you feel like your body carries parts of your story? Do you feel like there are things trapped inside of you?
4. In what ways has intensity shown up in your life? How have you learned to manage it? What does it feel like when your intensity is rejected by others?
5. Do you feel like you have access to your heart? What are some ways that you can engage your body in order to engage your heart?

Chapter 5

1. What has your relationship with your faith been like in the context of your Eightness? Do you feel like God relates with your anger or does he reject it?
2. What has revenge looked like in your life? Do you feel like you have a constant thirst for vengeance?
3. In what areas have you seen your anger go off the rails? Are you able to name people you have hurt with your anger?
4. What has betrayal looked like in your life? Do you believe there is a way to recover from it? What would that look like?
5. How would it feel to have someone else in charge? What might it look like to trust in God's provision and protection over your life rather than your own?

Chapter 6

1. Do you feel like it's easy to relate to other numbers? What has your experience been interacting with those different from you?
2. What numbers are your favorite to hang out with? What numbers do you feel safest with?
3. Which numbers are the hardest for you to get along with? Which numbers do you distrust the most?

4. Why is it hard to relate to some numbers?
5. What has been the most helpful thing you have learned in your relationships with other numbers?

Chapter 7
1. What has "imprinting" looked like in your relationships?
2. What has rejection looked like for you? Do you find yourself rejecting others before they can reject you?
3. How should someone approach you directly and honestly? Are there ways that they can do it where you won't be put on the defensive?
4. What has conflict looked like for you with those closest to you? What are the areas of conflict that have been the hardest?
5. What did you learn about yourself in relationships from this chapter? What is one tip you're going to press into and try out?

Chapter 8
1. What has stress and security looked like in your life? Were the Five and Two paradigms helpful?
2. What triangles do you have in your life? What triangles did you inherit from your family?
3. Where can you safely explore your weaknesses? How can you embrace your limits?
4. Do you have people that can hurt you? What would it look like to work through trust and betrayal with them?
5. Can you name your inner child with a word or image? What might it look like to become more in touch with that child?
6. What is your journey ahead? What are your action steps? What are the areas you want to work on?

APPENDIX B

I WAS RAISED BY AN EIGHT

This is a section that I considered putting in as one of the main chapters in the book.

However, since this chapter is more geared towards non-Eights than any of the others (even the marriage one), then I thought it might be helpful as an appendix.

Plus, I had decided on Eight chapters total for the book and I'm too damn stubborn to change my mind now.

Regardless, this is a fascinating chapter. One that I have often been very curious about.

What happens to those raised by Eights? What narratives do they learn? How bad does it get if their Eight parent is unhealthy?

I have scavenged the internet, other resources, and my many friends who have been raised by Eights to try and accurately portray what it might have been like.

Needless to say, most struggled with their Eight parents.

Eights usually impute onto their children that the world isn't safe. Parent Eights try to create little protectors who can fend for themselves.

Eights will often insert their passions into their children and want their child to be as committed to their passions as they are. They can frequently be too intense and insensitive to their children, while being a no-nonsense parent.

Because of forcing their kids to believe the world is scary, they often create fearful (or Enneagram Six) children who learn to rely on their Eight parent for protection–or they create rebellious (or counterphobic Six) children who rebel against them.

Children of Eights can struggle to find the self-confidence to save the world like their Eight parent does. This insufficiency compared to their parent creates quite a good amount of inner insecurity in the child.

I have a theory that Eight parents produce at least one Six child who then grows up and raises an Eight child of their own. This is at least true of my own story—my grandfather is an Eight, my dad is a Phobic Six, and I'm obviously another Eight.

However, not all of the Eight's children become Sixes. Many children become all the other types of the Enneagram. Sometimes even, an Eight produces another Eight in one of their children!

Talk about a shitstorm.

Regardless of what specific type you turned out to be, you probably have some shared experiences from your Eight parent. Often, Eight parents want to create kids who are strong warriors and have a strong identity. If your parent is an Eight, you have probably experienced this reality firsthand.

Let me tell you a story about this from Jackie, an Enneagram One who was raised by an Eight.

My dad is a really invested dad.

He wanted to coach all of the sports teams of my siblings and I growing up. He became the Parks and Rec basketball coach for my 6th grade team one year—filled with all my friends of varying athletic abilities.

I'm sure he was a great coach that season and helped us further our basketball skills, but I don't remember any of that. I only remember one part of that season during a practice one night.

We were doing some sort of shooting and running drill where if we missed a free throw, we would have to run laps together as a team. Well, we missed a bunch of shots and proceeded to run around and around the court.

One of my friends, Karly, had asthma and started having a small asthma attack. He thought she was just trying to get out of running so he yelled at us all to keep going. I ended up having to plead with him to let her stop so that she could catch her breath.

This memory stands out in my mind because I really shouldn't have to advocate for my friend in the midst of a 6th grade basketball practice. But, coach dad was set on whipping us into shape!

He had the intensity of a collegiate level coach without the understanding that we were actually just 12-year-old girls.

He operates with this level of intensity often—which I appreciated a lot through childhood! He gets things done and cares a lot. But, I often found myself wishing he would tone it down, look around, and proceed with caution.

I'm sure that many of you who were raised by Eights can relate to Jackie's story.

You can relate to the intensity, the demanding and commanding presence, and the lack of awareness of their impact on you and those around them.

When Eights are healthy, this impact can be life giving and empowering to their children. When Eights are unhealthy, this impact can be devastating.

This was certainly true of Steve's relationship with his father, Pete.

When Steve was 8, his Eight father Pete enrolled him in some jujitsu classes.

In order to prepare for this, Pete would make Steve do 50 push-ups every night and workout after class.

Pete thought that these classes would prepare his fragile son for the world. Pete figured it was time Steve grew up and fought back. It was time for Steve to become a man.

At Steve's first match, his whole family came out to watch him, including his father Pete. Unfortunately, Steve was losing to the other kid pretty badly. Yet, Steve remembered his dad's words and kept trying.

Eventually as he kept losing, Steve broke and started to cry on the mat.

For Pete, this was unacceptable. Their family was not wussies. Their family fought back; they didn't cry in front of everyone.

So, Pete got up from his seat in the bleachers and yelled at his son, "You're embarrassing the family! Toughen up!"

With this, Pete left the gym out of disgust.

This is often the reality of children of Eights.

Your Eight parent treated you too strongly. They expected too much of you. They demanded you to be strong. They might have even taken their anger out on you.

Whatever your situation was like growing up with an Eight, I am certain that adulthood has been an interesting journey for you.

How does one interact with a strong parental figure once they themselves are also an adult? Is it even possible to grow close to an Eight parent? Are all kids of Eights doomed?

I am not sure what the answers are to those questions. I wish there was an easy guidebook to reconciliation and relationships with parents once you become an adult. I wish more Eight parents did the work of becoming softer humans.

For anyone, navigating your relationship with your parents is a hard and delicate task. For those raised by Eights, it can be an excruciating one.

Eight parents often refuse to admit wrongdoing from your childhood. They might tell you that they did the best they could. They tried to help. They thought they were preparing you for life.

It might be hard to ever receive a genuine apology from your Eight parent.

As with all that we have learned about Eights so far in this book, there is hope.

There's hope for the nastiest of Eight parents. There's hope for the toughest of Eight parents. There's hope for you and your relationship with them.

The hope may not be huge. It might not ever come to fruition. But, I believe that Eights can be softened. They can learn to admit weakness and mistakes. They can learn to let their hearts lead rather than their anger.

Maybe step one is asking your Eight parent about their own childhood and what that was like for them. Maybe it's starting by sharing your desire to grow in your relationship and start afresh. Maybe even, it's getting your Eight parent read this book.

Whatever it is, I have hope for your relationship with your Eight parent. I believe there is always time and opportunity to start anew. I genuinely hope you can heal from your wounds.

For those of you whose Eight parent has already passed away, I hope that this book brought some level of understanding and context for why they were the way that they were to you. I know it doesn't change anything about your childhood, but maybe this language and understanding can bring closure in some way.

As with anything, as with any Eight, as with any human, it is so important that you allow yourself to feel the things you felt from childhood being raised by an Eight. To not let them gaslight you into their version of events. To not let them dismiss or demean your pain. But, to simply acknowledge and accept that what happened is what happened.

Your Eight parent was the way they were. Your pain from childhood is what it is. Those memories and things did happen. I believe you.

It is only from here that you can find healing, restoration, and peace in your journey, whether that is with your Eight parent or not.

I hope this book brought you understanding about your Eight parent or guardian. If nothing else, at least you understand why they were an asshole.

APPENDIX C

88 IMPERATIVES FOR EIGHTS

These are in no particular order.

When writing this book, there wasn't space to just offer one-off action steps. Here is the culmination of all of those.

Take a year and do one of these a day–repeat the ones that were especially challenging.

1. Slow down
2. Know that the cure for the pain is in the pain
3. Reach out to your childhood friends and ask them to introduce you to your childhood self–notice the difference between their descriptions and your own perception
4. Journal
5. Learn how to actually rest
6. Don't be afraid of counseling–I know you aren't, but just in case
7. When people misunderstand you and call you names, don't attack them–it'll only increase their false perception of you
8. Get an emotions wheel and practice naming emotions other than anger
9. Discover that feedback is painful but it's worth it
10. Be intentionally unproductive and see what happens
11. Slow down
12. Listen to others without having to offer input

13. Pursue gentleness and kindness with the same ferocity and intensity you pursue other things
14. Take a walk instead of working out
15. Embrace your inner child–be compassionate to them
16. Notice your intensity and reduce your impulsiveness to respond
17. Believe that those around you are not trying to harm or betray you, even when it feels like that
18. Learn the beauty of moderacy, balance, and limits
19. Explore where your heart breaks in the world–you might find your own story behind those things
20. Get a rescue dog
21. Slow the fuck down
22. Realize that you don't need to be provocative to be loved
23. Learn to pause, especially when emotionally flared up
24. Learn to say no to commitments–take a season and say no to almost everything
25. Question your instincts
26. Try to receive love and give love more openly
27. Find peers–You are good at being under and above people, learn to submit and rely on peers
28. Be aware of the space you take up in a room or relationship
29. Don't interrupt people – even if they're rambling, let them finish
30. Stop strategizing to protect yourself–loss of control can actually lead to relief not hurt.
31. Slow down, dammit
32. Press into your heart–be compassionate towards the softer sides of you
33. Learn how to stop the fight and back down
34. Stop trying to save and protect the world
35. Write down a list of your core positive and negative memories and notice patterns
36. Find safe people who can calibrate your Eightness
37. Enjoy the present, don't plan ahead or look behind
38. Get a full body massage
39. Discover the difference between transparency and vulnerability
40. Please slow down, bitch
41. Find a group of people you trust and stick with them
42. Discover the words that others use against you that piss you off and be curious about it

43. Grow in patience
44. Make a list of all the people you hold grudges against and figure out how to forgive them
45. Make a list of all the people you've hurt and figure out how to ask for forgiveness
46. Realize the beauty in not having to win every argument, fight, or competition
47. Set reasonable expectations for yourself and others
48. Realize the difference between your passion & aggression
49. Pause before confronting or critiquing someone
50. Identify when you are fighting because you feel anxious or unsafe and find a different way to respond to it
51. SLOW the Fuck Down
52. Ask people how they perceive you and trust them
53. Ask people how they hear your words and listen
54. Ask people how you come across and change
55. Ask people what your impact is, compare it with your intentions, and then adjust
56. Just fucking ask people about yourself and listen to them, dammit
57. Take care of your body and your diet
58. Take all of the personality tests and strengths finders–learn things from them, even if they're mostly bullshit
59. Write down a list of your life's priorities and live accordingly
60. Find stillness
61. SLOW THE FUCK DOWN
62. If you're self-preservation repressed, decorate your home and take care of yourself
63. If you're social repressed, join a group or club and find some identity in it
64. If you're sexual repressed, set aside specific time to be with trusted ones and be truly open to them
65. Do something you're not good at
66. Get your anger out through working out
67. Hang out with kids and populations that you don't find "powerful" or "threatening"
68. Do yoga and deep breathing exercises
69. If you're an Eight wing Seven, learn impulse control and delayed gratification

70. If you're an Eight wing Nine, learn to find places to explore your anger so you don't explode
71. It's time to slow down
72. If you're ever angry or anxious, workout first before you go and do something about it
73. When you're in a relationship, learn the beauty of not responding in the heat of the moment
74. Be aware of moments you feel overwhelmed (anxious) and dive underneath those feelings to the root narratives
75. Workout until you cry
76. Discover that not getting what you want from loved ones isn't betrayal
77. Set aside a weekly time with your loved ones to process your emotions, unresolved conflicts, and sync up
78. Don't assume that honesty is always what others need
79. When you feel the urge to tell someone to "fuck off," pause and breathe for 10 seconds
80. Find those who are willing to stay in the fight with you
81. Slowing down is super important, but it's also okay to run full speed sometimes
82. Learn to receive intimacy in its various forms, especially in the less intense versions
83. Not everyone is out to get you, stop thinking and acting that way
84. Use your friends to help you see your blind spots
85. When you feel betrayed or misunderstood by someone, take it to your trusted friends who know you best and let them sort tell you what's true and untrue
86. Stop lying, just admit you're wrong when you are
87. Do the work
88. Be an Eight, the world needs it

APPENDIX D

MUSIC, MOVIES, AND FAMOUS EIGHTS

I have found that discovering media and figures that represent Eights have been immensely helpful in my journey towards health.

We can listen to music that engages the deep well of emotions Eights have. We can watch movies that simulate our own lives in parallel narratives. We can look to Eight figures–historical and fictional–to learn from them.

I hope these lists bless you as they have blessed me.

Music

You can find the whole playlist on Spotify under "I'm An 8-Hole - The Enneagram 8 Playlist."

It is over eight hours of vulgar, tender, goodness that I still regularly update with new Eight-like songs. I recommend playing all of these songs at full volume.

Movies

This is a list of 30 movies or movie series from the last 50 years. It is not exhaustive by any means.

Some of these movies are on here because one of their main characters is an Eight. Others are on here because they touch on important themes related to being an Eight.

Alita Battle Angel (2019)	Good Will Hunting (1997)	Scarface (1983)
Brave (2012)	Gran Torino (2008)	Schindler's List (1993)
Braveheart (1995)	Hellboy 1 & 2 (2004, 2008)	Selma (2014)
Captain Marvel (2019)	The Hunger Games (2012-2015)	Taken (2008)
Cruella (2021)	The Incredibles (2004)	Training Day (2001)
Django Unchained (2012)	Kill Bill Volume 1 & 2 (2003-2004)	Warrior (2011)
Fifty Shades of Grey (2015-2018)	Lara Croft: Tomb Raider (2001)	Whiplash (2014)
Flight (2012)	Mad Max: Fury Road (2015)	Wolverine (2013)
Gladiator (2000)	Malcom and Marie (2021)	10 Things I Hate About You (1999)
The Godfather (1972)	Promising Young Woman (2020)	300 (2006)

Famous Eights

It is remarkably hard to type characters and people.

So, if you disagree with any of these, that's fine. This list is the best that my brain, my fellow Eight friends, and the internet could supply us.

This is the most comprehensive list I've seen in existence so you're welcome.

Historical	Fictional
Al Sharpton (Minister and Activist)	Achilles (The Iliad)
Alfred Nobel (Scientist)	Agamemnon (The Odyssey)
Alec Baldwin (Actor)	Alanna (The Song of the Lioness)
Alex Jones (Political Commentator)	Alastor Moody (Harry Potter Series)
Alexander Hamilton (American Revolutionary)	Alice Nakiri (Food Wars)
Alexandria Ocasio Cortez (Politician)	Alita (Alita Battle Angel)
Ali Wong (Comedian)	Anger (Inside Out)
Andrew Cuomo (Politician)	Archie (Pokémon)
Andrew Johnson (U.S. President)	Arya Stark (Game of Thrones)
Ares (God of War)	Askeladd (Vinland Saga)
Aretha Franklin (Musician)	Astrid Hofferson (How To Train Your Dragon)
Aurelian (Roman Emperor)	Asuka Langley Soryu (Neon Genesis Evangelion)
Barbara Walters (News Anchor)	Azula (Avatar The Last Airbender)
Barnabas (New Testament)	Bane (The Dark Knight Rises
Barry Bonds (Professional Baseball Player)	Beast (Beauty and the Beast)
Benito Mussolini (Prime Minister of Italy)	Beth Pearson (This Is Us)
Bhad Bhabie (Musician and Influencer)	Biff Tannen (Back to the Future)
Bill Maher (Political Commentator)	Bill (Kill Bill)
Bruce Lee (Actor)	Bill Cypher (Gravity Falls)
Caligula (Roman Emperor)	Bowser (Super Mario)
Candace Owens (Political Commentator)	Britta Perry (Community)
Caravaggio (Italian Painter)	Bryan Mills (Taken)
Charles Barkley (NBA Player)	Buttercup (Powerpuff Girls)
Charlize Theron (Actress)	Carl Lightman (Lie To Me)
Chelsea Handler (Comedian)	Carla Tortelli (Cheers)
Chevy Chase (Actor)	Captain Leonard Burns (Fire Force)
Chris Hemsworth (Actor)	Captain Marvel (Captain Marvel)
Christopher Columbus (Explorer and Colonizer)	Carly Shannon (Travelers)
Chuck Liddell (Professional Fighter)	Carrie Heffernan (King of Queens)
Clint Eastwood (Actor and Director	Casey Gardner (Atypical)

Coco Chanel (French Fashion Designer)	Cassie Thomas (Promising Young Woman)
Connor McGregor (Professional Fighter)	CeCe Parekh (New Girl)
Courtney Love (Musician/Actress)	Cersei Lannister (Game of Thrones)
Cornel West (Philosopher and Activist)	Christian Grey (Fifty Shades of Grey)
Curtis James Jackson III (50 Cent)	Christopher Robin (Winnie The Pooh)
Danny DeVito (Actor)	Chuck Bass (Gossip Girl)
Dave Bautista (Actor)	Colonel Walter W. Kurtz (Apocalypse Now)
Dave Portnoy (Sports Commentator)	Creon (Antigone)
Dave Ramsey (Financial Expert)	Cruella De Vil (Cruella)
Dean Martin (Musician)	Daenerys Targaryen (Game of Thrones)
Denzel Washington (Actor)	Damon Salvatore (Vampire Diaries)
Diego Maradona (Professional Soccer Player)	Darkseid (DC Universe)
Diogenes (Greek Philosopher)	Darth Maul (Star Wars)
DMX (Musician)	Darth Vader (Star Wars)
Donald Trump (U.S. President)	Debbie Thornberry (The Wild Thornberry's)
Dr. Dre (Musician and Producer)	Dee Reynolds (Always Sunny in Philadelphia)
Dr. Martin Luther King Jr. (Reverend and Activist)	Donna Meagle (Parks and Rec)
Dr. Phil (Talk Show Host)	Donna Pinciotti (That 70's Show)
Duane Chapman (Bounty Hunter)	Dorothy Zbornak (Golden Girls)
Eazy-E (Musician)	Dr. Gregory House (House)
Elijah (Old Testament)	Dr. Stranger (Marvel, Could be a Three)
Ernest Hemmingway (Author)	Dr. Temperance Brennan (Bones)
Fidel Castro (Prime Minister of Cuba)	Dracula (Dracula)
Francis Ford Coppola (Movie Director)	Drax The Destroyer (Marvel)
Frank Sinatra (Musician)	Edward Rochester (Jane Eyre)
Franklin D. Roosevelt (U.S. President)	Elaine Benes (Seinfeld)
Genghis Khan (Emperor of Mongol Empire)	Eleanor Shellstop (The Good Place)
George Patton (U.S. General)	Elizabeth Bennet (Pride and Prejudice - could be Seven Wing Eight)
George Soros (Businessman)	Elizabeth Swan (Pirates of the Caribbean)
Goliath (Old Testament)	Emily Gilmore (Gilmore Girls)
Gordon Ramsey	Emperor Palpatine (Star Wars)

(Professional Chef)	
Hannibal (Roman General)	Endeavor (My Hero Academia)
Henry Ford (Businessman)	Eowyn (Lord of the Rings)
Henry VIII (England Monarch)	Eric Cartman (South Park)
Indira Gandhi (Prime Minister of India)	Eris Boreas Greyrat (Mushoku Tensei)
Ivan The Terrible (Grand Prince of Moscow)	Esmeralda (Hunchback of Notre Dame)
Jair Bolsonaro (President of Brazil)	Frank Castle (The Punisher)
James Hetfield (Musician)	Frank Underwood (House of Cards)
Jason Statham (Actor)	Franziska Doppler (Dark)
Jay Z (Musician)	Gamora (Guardians of the Galaxy)
Jennifer Hudson (Musician)	Ganondorf (The Legend Of Zelda)
Jessi (Musician)	Gendo Ikari (Neon Genesis Evangelion)
Joan Jett (Musician)	Gimli (Lord of the Rings)
Joe Rogan (Talk Show Host)	Ginny Weasley (Harry Potter Books, not Movies)
Joseph Stalin (Leader of Soviet Union)	Gon Freecs (Hunter X Hunter)
John Gotti (Mafia Boss)	Green Goblin (Spiderman)
John McCain (Politician)	Hades (Hadestown)
John the Baptist (New Testament)	Hank Schrader (Breaking Bad)
John Wayne (Actor)	Hans (Frozen)
Johnny Cash (Musician)	Harvey Specter (Suits)
Karl Malone (Professional Basketball Player)	Hector Barbosa (Pirates of the Caribbean)
Katharine Hepburn (Actor)	Helga Pataki (Hey Arnold!)
Kathy Bates (Actress)	Hellboy (Hellboy)
Khabib Nurmagomedov (Professional Fighter)	Hugo Stigletts (Inglorious Bastards)
Kim Jong-un (North Korea Leader)	Inosuke Hashibara (Demon Slayer)
Laura Ingraham (Political Commentator)	Inspector Javert (Les Misérables)
Lauren Bacall (Actress)	Jabba the Hut (Star Wars)
Lil Wayne (Musician)	Jack Baur (24)
Lucille Ball (Actress)	Jack Merridew (Lord of the Flies)
Lucy Liu (Actress)	James "Sawyer" Ford (Lost)
Mark Cuban (Businessman)	Jang Deok-Su (Squid Game)
Mark Driscoll (Evangelical Pastor)	Jasmine (Aladdin)
Mark McGwire (Professional Baseball Player)	Jason Dean (Heathers)
Marlon Brando (Actor)	Jason Street (Friday Night Lights)

Megan Thee Stallion (Musician)	Jay Pritchett (Modern Family)
Mike Ditka (Professional Football Player)	Jeanie Matthews (Divergent)
Missy Elliot (Musician)	Jen Harding (Dead to Me)
Miriam (Old Testament)	Jessica Jones (Marvel's Jessica Jones)
Mother Teresa (Saint and Nun– People think she was a Two, but she's a Social Eight)	Jessie (Pokémon)
Muammar Gaddafi (Libya Leader)	Jim Hopper (Stranger Things)
Muhammad Ali (Professional Fighter)	Jiren (Dragon Ball Super)
Naomi Campbell (Supermodel)	Jo March (Little Women)
Napoleon Bonaparte (French Military Leader)	Johanna Mason (Hunger Games Series)
Nebuchadnezzar II (Babylonian King)	John Bender (Breakfast Club)
Nick Saban (Football Coach)	John Creasy (Man on Fire)
Notorious BIG (Musician)	John Locke (Lost)
Pablo Picasso (Spanish Painter)	John Luther (Luther)
Patrice O'Neal (Comedian)	Karma Akabane (Assassination Classroom)
Pink (Musician)	Kat Stratford (10 Things I Hate About You)
Queen Latifa (Actress)	Kate Bishop (Hawkeye)
Ramani Durvasula (Psychologist)	Katniss Everdeen (Hunger Games)
Randy Jackson (Musician)	Katsuki Bakugo (My Hero Academia)
Recep Erdogan (Turkey President)	Kelsier (Mistborn)
Reuven Rivlin (Israeli President)	Khan Noonien Singh (Star Trek)
Rick Ross (Musician)	Killmonger (Black Panther)
Ridley Scott (Producer)	Kingpin (Daredevil)
Robert Duvall (Actor)	Klaus Mikaelson (Vampire Diaries)
Roseanne Barr (Comedian)	Korra (Legend of Korra)
Rush Limbaugh (Political Commentator)	Kyo Kusanagi (The King of Fighters)
Rosie O'Donnell (Comedian)	Lara Croft (Tomb Raider)
Russel Crowe (Actor)	Lelouch Lamperouge (Code Geass)
Saddam Hussein (Iraqi President)	Leonidas (300)
Salma Hayek (Actress)	Lionel Luthor (Smallville)
Samson (Old Testament)	Llewelyn Moss (No Country for Old Men)
Samuel L. Jackson (Actor)	Lucy van Pelt (Peanuts)
Sandra Bullock (Actress - might be Nine wing Eight)	Luke Cage (Luke Cage)
Sandra Oh (Actress)	Lynette Scavo (Desperate Housewives)
Sean Penn (Actor)	Madame Thenardier (Les Misérables)
Serena Williams (Professional	Madara Uchiha (Naruto)

Tennis Player)	
Shin Ryujin (Musician)	Maeve Wiley (Sex Education)
Socrates (Greek Philosopher)	Magneto (X-Men)
Steve Balmer (Businessman and NBA Owner)	Malcolm (Malcom and Marie)
Steve Bannon (Political Strategist)	Matt Murdock (Daredevil)
Steve Jobs (Creator of Apple)	Maui (Moana)
Susan Sarandon (Actress)	Max Mayfield (Stranger Things)
Theodore Roosevelt (U.S. President)	Maximus (Gladiator)
Tim Raue (Professional Chef)	Megara (Hercules)
Thomas Paine (Political Theorist)	Megatron (Transformers)
Tom Hardy (Actor)	Meruem (Hunter x Hunter)
Toni Morrison (Author)	Merida (Brave)
Tony Bennett (Musician)	Michael Myers (Halloween)
Tupac Shakur (Musician)	Mike Ehrmantraut (Breaking Bad)
Vince Lombardi (Professional Football Coach)	Miranda Priestly (The Devil Wears Prada)
Vince McMahon (Owner of WWE)	Monkey D. Luffy (One Piece)
Vladimir Putin (Russian President–Could be a Counterphobic Six)	Mr. Glass (Glass)
Walt Disney (Found of Disney)	Mufasa (Lion King)
Winston Churchill (U.K. Prime Minister)	Nandor the Relentless (What We Do in the Shadows)
Xi Jingping (Chinese Leader)	Nate Jacobs (Euphoria)
Zeus (God of Thunder)	Negan (The Walking Dead)
Zlatan Ibrahimovic (Professional Soccer Player)	Nick Fury (Avengers)
6ix9ine (Musician)	Nobara Kugisaki (Jujutsu Kaisen)
21 Savage (Musician)	Number Five (The Umbrella Academy)
Fictional (Continued)	**Fictional (Continued)**
Odin Borson (Marvel)	Stanley Hudson (The Office)
Oliver Queen (Arrow)	Stevie Budd (Schitt's Creek)
Olivia Pope (Scandal)	Stewie Griffin (Family Guy)
Patty Hewes (Damages)	Sukuna (Jujutsu Kaisen)
Plankton (SpongeBob SquarePants)	Susie Green (Curb Your Enthusiasm)
President Coin (Hunger Games Series)	Susie Myerson (Marvelous Mrs. Maisel)
Princess Leia (Star Wars)	Tezzeret (Magic: The Gathering)
Professor Callahan (Legally Blonde)	Thanos (Avengers End Game)
Queen of Hearts (Alice in	The Horned King (The Black Cauldron)

Wonderland)	
Ragnar Lothbrok (Vikings)	The Master (Dr. Who)
Ragyo Kiryuin (Kill La Kill)	Theo Crain (Haunting of Hill House)
Ratigan (The Great Mouse Detective)	Thors Snorresson (Vinland Saga)
Re-L Mayer (Ergo Proxy)	Tigress (Kung Fu Panda)
Rhett Butler (Gone with the Wind)	Tom Conlon (Warrior)
Rin Okumura (Blue Exorcist)	Tommy Shelby (Peaky Blinders)
Robin Scherbatsky (How I Met Your Mother)	Toni Shalifoe (The Wilds)
Roronoa Zoro (One Piece)	Tony Montana (Scarface)
Rocket (Guardians of the Galaxy)	Tony Soprano (The Sopranos)
Rosa Diaz (Brooklyn 99)	Tony Stark (Iron Man, could be a Three)
Roy Kent (Ted Lasso)	Toph Beifong (Avatar the Last Airbender)
Roy Mustang (Fullmetal Alchemist)	Tuco Salamanca (Breaking Bad)
Roz Doyle (Frasier)	Tyler Durden (Fight Club)
Sam Puckett (iCarly)	Tywin Lannister (Game of Thrones)
Santana Lopez (Glee)	Valkyrie (Marvel)
Sara Lance (Arrow)	Vanitas (Case Study of Vanitas)
Selina Kyle "Catwoman" (The Batman)	Vicky (The Fairly Odd Parents)
Shadow (Sonic)	Vito Corleone (The Godfather)
Shan Yu (Mulan)	Voldemort (Harry Potter - Could be a One)
Shere Khan (Mowgli)	Wanda Maximoff (Marvel, could be a Nine wing Eight)
Shiki Tademaru (Kemono Jihen)	Xena (Xena: Warrior Princess)
Sirius Black (Harry Potter)	Yennefer (The Witcher)
Skipper (Madagascar)	Yusuke Urameshi (Yu Hakusho)
Slade (Teen Titans Go!)	Zabuza (Naruto)
Spirit (Spirit: Stallion of the Cimarron)	Zeek Braverman (Parenthood)

Acknowledgements

This book would not have come to fruition without the support, encouragement, and love from myself.

Just kidding, I am not that arrogant. There are plenty of people to thank here.

Namely, thank you to my own mother who spent hours editing this work for grammar, syntax, and content. I couldn't imagine reading a book from my own son where he talks candidly about his childhood wounds and still being able to push through all of it to edit for him. You are the real MVP, Momma.

Thank you to Kale Daniels, who created the cover art for this book. Kale, I am thankful for your patience and creativity in helping me design this cover. I truly would not have been able to do it without you.

Outside of this, thank you to all my friends who were the guinea pigs with this project. To the many Eights who read along, to my faithful Enneagram Two friend, Taylor, who put more hours in than most everyone combined, and to the rest of my friends who read 55,000 words of an unfinished book on an Enneagram number that they don't even identify with. You are all incredible.

Furthermore, I want to thank my mentor and friend Chad. Chad, our monthly calls to talk through life in the context of the Eight has changed my life. We have journeyed through tragedies, deaths, joys, triumphs, and many marathons (all on your end). Our conversations have given me language and depth to my own story that I would not have found elsewhere. Thank you for being the second father that every Eight needs.

Above all, thank you to all of you who have walked through the last year with me:

To the people in my house church, thank you for allowing me to be just a normal and beloved person again, and not the lonely pastor I used to be.

To my close friends here in Seattle: Sam, Taylor, Naveen, Trent, Riley, Taylor, Abbie, Sabrina, Levi, Caleb, Mike, Mary Jean, my family, and more. Thank you for letting me have PTSD flashbacks and be safe with each of you.

To Ryan Broushet, Jake Nagy, Jeremy Lupinacci, and Ryan Hiney, thank you for talking with me monthly and encouraging me to continue on this journey towards health as an Eight.

To my therapist Jim, thank you for helping me overcome PTSD and face my fears.

To Jesus, thank you for showing me that the path to true life comes through death. The cross has become my metaphor for this season.

I have never had to rely on more people in my life than I have recently. This has truly been the toughest year of my life, but also the most beautiful year to date.

I could not have made it without each of you and your support.

Peace,
C.V. Meo

References

Books on the Enneagram:

Chestnut, B. (2013). *The Complete Enneagram: 27 Paths to Greater Self-Knowledge* (Illustrated ed.). She Writes Press.

Cron, I. M., & Stabile, S. (2016). *The Road Back to You: An Enneagram Journey to Self-Discovery*. IVP Books.

McCord, B., & McCord, J. (2019). *Becoming Us: Using the Enneagram to Create a Thriving Gospel-Centered Marriage*. Morgan James Publishing.

Palmer, H. (1995). *The Enneagram in Love and Work: Understanding Your Intimate and Business Relationships* (1st ed.). HarperOne.

Riso, D. R., & Hudson, R. (1999). *The Wisdom of the Enneagram: The Complete Guide to Psychological and Spiritual Growth for the Nine Personality Types* (Illustrated ed.). Bantam.

Rohr, R., & Ebert, A. (2001). *The Enneagram: A Christian Perspective* (Illustrated ed.). Crossroad.

Thomson, C. (2002). *Parables and the Enneagram*. Ninestar Publishing.

Made in the USA
Columbia, SC
18 April 2024